GRANDPA, YOU WERE RIGHT

MAN IS RUINING HIS OWN NEST

BY
CARI PALMER

Copyright © 2023 Cari Palmer

All rights reserved.

No portion of this book may be reproduced in any form without written permission from the publisher or author except as permitted by U.S. copyright law.

For Liam and Jonathan

Stacie thank you for trusting the importance of the Bridge.

TABLE OF CONTENTS

Chapter 1 The Ten Commandments 2
Chapter 2 Purple People Parable 7
Chapter 3 Seven Months Ago – "Before" 9
Chapter 4 Who Do I Think I Am 15
Chapter 5 Answering My Calling 19
Chapter 6 Through An Enlightened Lens 22
Chapter 7 Our Mission On This Rock 30
Chapter 8 Take Me To Your Leader 36
Chapter 9 Bopa 41
Chapter 10 Simpler Times 43
Chapter 11 Living In Search Mode 47
Chapter 12 Coddled/ Sensitive Kids 49
Chapter 13 They Want To Work. You Make It Hell 57
Chapter 14 Love. Marriage. Relationships. 60
Chapter 15 Making Babies 77
Chapter 16 Having A Leg Up 83
Chapter 17 Programming 89
Chapter 18 The Dentist 100
Chapter 19 Say 'Yes' To You 102
Chapter 20 Writer's Strike 108
Chapter 21 Remember Equal Footing? 111
Chapter 22 Man Is Ruining His Own Nest 122
Chapter 23 Respect 125
Chapter 24 Purple People Update 127

Chapter 25 Untangling Backwards Beliefs.................128

Chapter 26 The Panel Channel 135

Chapter 27 WWJD...138

Chapter 28 You Are The Problem 147

Chapter 29 Paving A New Way 165

Chapter 30 You Live Like Christ?.............................168

Chapter 31 My Least Favorite Thing... Politics.........173

Chapter 32 Preplanned Consciousness Events 186

Chapter 33 Self Imposed Significant People 187

Chapter 34 Early Cruise Journal Entries 193

Chapter 35 Puerto Vallarta Fearlessly 200

Chapter 35 Mazatlan Gave Me Hope 206

Chapter 36 The Ship Story 212

Chapter 37 We've Become Insignificant....................225

Chapter 38 Journaling Continued – New Lens..........232

Chapter 39 Why I Went To Maui 240

Chapter 40 Cruise Afterburn 244

Chapter 41 Laying The Foundation 249

Chapter 42 Purple People Epilogue 255

PART ONE

Can you imagine yourself enjoying life and having fun at the expense of someone else's pain? Of course not. That is not who you are. You would never experience pleasure if you knew somebody was suffering because of it.

You are not who you think you are.

This book is for you because until now, you had no idea that you don't know who you are. Take your time reading this book. When you feel anger, stop! What was triggered? **Find the triggers** *and you will find the way to who you came here to be. You can direct your anger at me, but that just delays your healing. I am just a messenger. You don't even know me. How can you be angry at me? What hurts your insides are the answers you are looking for. Journal as you move along. Welcome home. I bet you missed you.*

CHAPTER 1
THE TEN COMMANDMENTS

If you don't know me yet, I've never attended church. We had no religion.

Because you've forgotten them; a reminder. This is my take on something you all have always known. Of course, you live by them. Right?

The Ten Commandments Re-Explained Cari's Way:

Thou shalt have no other gods before me

Meaning the only way to God is through your higher knowing. Not through someone or something else. Not through somebody else translating their version of God to you. God speaks to you in a way only you can hear. When you hear God through somebody else, it triggers ickiness. It's not the right version for you. You have your own download. Listen to it.

Refrain from spiritual materialism. You don't need any or all of those objects that you believe have special powers. All the power you need is within you. The crystals are pretty, but not necessary.

Thou shalt not take the name of the Lord thy God in vain

Humans use this word interestingly. If you put your hand on a Bible and you swear to God, they can't wait to hold it against you. They call this a sin. There are no sins. Sometimes we have to do things against our better judgment, but we know the way. If we listen to our higher self, we always know what to do. If someone is offended by your action, it is not what you did. It is something within them. Words mean nothing. Intention means everything. You can't know what's going on inside of any other body. Stop looking outward and look inside. What they trigger in you is what you need to repair.

Remember the Sabbath Day, to keep it holy

God did not want you to gather with your friends and family and sit inside a box on Sunday. He did not want you to gossip about your neighbors or what's going on in town. This is not holy. Holy time means reserving at least one day for introspect if you can't do it all the time. Find one day to find peace within yourself. Put everything else away. Let everything and everyone else go. Be one with you. This is the time to reconnect with God. God suggested a weekly practice. You don't do it at all.

It was not meant to be a day where you watch football, have barbeques and pool parties, golf, or hang out with others. It is meant as a time when you go into nature and connect with God. Let the elders take the children to the box as you take this space to heal what aches within your soul.

You allowed your day of God to be taken up by things that are more interesting to you. **Find a time that works for you.** It is your time to be alone. Time for only you and your higher-self to connect to all that is. This time is what takes you back to God. You cannot get there when you are with others. It is a solo soul experience. Get back into this solo-soul-excursion practice. See where it takes you. Re-member why you came here.

Do not go to a room full of people and check the box that you did your God work for the week. It is a private practice. You cannot hear Him unless you are listening. You don't know how to listen.

Honor thy father and mother

Means honoring and respecting people who have been here longer than you have. Help those who are in need and be a God-servant on the street.

As this is written, it is directed to the generation who has yet to learn how to function. We have a layer of young humans who have much learning to do. They believe they are the answers.

Respect experience and wisdom. Do not take anything on as a 'belief' in the process. Allow life experience to show you what is true. Much wisdom is contained within decades of life. We learn as we grow. Honor the elders. Talk to them, learn from them. Leave your children with them.

Do not reinvent the wheel unless you have to.

Thou shalt not murder

You cannot murder if you do not feel anger. If you feel anger growing inside of you, trust that you have stayed inside of a story for too long. It is time to leave. When you walk away from the situation you will no longer have the emotion that you attached to it. Walk away and look at it from the lens of an outsider. This is where you can see how you participated in creating the madness that allowed the anger to sink in.

Have no expectations of others because they are on their journey. They will always let you down. We all must let everyone down. We cannot be what you need us to be and be who we are supposed to be at the same time. They cannot fit into your reality because you want them too. Trust that their story is equally as important as yours. Set them free. Move on. Give them the grace to do the same.

Thou shalt not commit adultery

Be in a relationship when you feel tingles and butterflies with the other person. When you both continually grow these feelings, you will remain together and faithful because you are happy. When the happy begins to fade, it is time to move on. Speak the truth to your partner. They already know. When the feelings of craving one another no longer exist, it is time to exit the story. You have run out of happy. Your time has come to move on. Be without a partner. Do not confuse love for need.

Push outside of the fear of the unknown and move on with your life. Do not stay in an ended relationship because leaving is hard. This is why we talk. When we don't, we can't know where the other person is. Know when to go. Don't be complacent. This is your lifetime. Spend it wisely.

Marriage is a creation of humans. It's for you to claim something as your own. Allow relationships to flow naturally. That is what they are supposed to do. People will come and go in your life. Don't get stuck in one story. It is not what God wanted. God did not want to create an industry around you loving someone. When it's over, it's over. It doesn't need to be drug through the mud.

Thou shalt not steal

Earn it. Build it. Create it. Work for it. Exchange for it.

Thou shalt not bear false witness against your neighbor.

The truth shall set you free. Be able to look yourself in the mirror and know that who you see is a beautiful person. A soul who knows 'what I do to you, you do to me. What I give to you, you give to me.'

You don't have to like anybody. But you do have to be respectful to them. If they do not show respect to you, be respectful to them. They have to live with themselves. You are the only one you have to live with.

You shalt not covet your neighbor's wife, or servant, or ox, or donkey, or anything that belongs to your neighbor.

If it belongs to your neighbor, it does not belong to you. Leave it alone. Find yours as it awaits you ahead.

CHAPTER 2
PURPLE PEOPLE PARABLE

Long ago in a village far, far away, lived a couple on the fringe of the village. They couldn't live inside the walls as they could not afford the taxes in the kingdom. She was pregnant. Everyone in the kingdom was encouraged to deliver children in the Kingdom's birth center. There was a medical team on hand if needed. They were open to all. When they entered the hospital, they saw the queen and her court coming in. She was also very pregnant and ready to deliver.

Everyone in the kingdom was a faint shade of purple. You really couldn't tell anyone apart, other than what they wore. After the babies were born, the poor man went into the nursery to see his child. He noticed the child nearby who was also wrapped in a blanket, but this cloth glittered with gold threads.

The man knew exactly what he had to do at that moment. He wrapped his baby in the golden cloth. He then put the royal baby in his basket. When they took the babies home, he told his wife what he did. She was elated. They knew now by having royal blood, this child stood a chance. They stood a chance. It would know how to lead them to abundance. This child could be the answer they needed for survival. They knew this would be a miracle.

As time went by, they knew all they could do to let the royal highness of this child evolve was to feed it, keep it safe and warm, and alive. They were going to let the child explore, discover, play, and do whatever came naturally. As the years went by, they started to second-guess their decision. They didn't see anything coming out of this kid that showed an ounce of royal blood. It was acting like a normal kid, but a kid without punishment or expectations. He was allowed to be whatever he was and follow things that he was curious about. Did they make a mistake? They knew there was nothing they could do about it. The choice was made at birth.

The day came when they went into town to witness the royal parade. They were excited to see what their child became. They figured they would see some cave-kid, dragging weird toys while walking in line with the Royals. What they saw, they could not believe. Their child was standing in line next to the other children. You almost could not tell them apart. Did they have any idea that standing next to them was a stupid kid with no potential whatsoever? Although their child looked wonderful on the outside, the parents knew who was inside that royalty costume. Of course, they could never say a word to anyone.

Where you are when you read this story says a lot about what you're getting out of the story. Write down what you believe before you start this adventure with me. You will be surprised by what you learn.

Which baby do you think is better off?

Which baby do you think has a better start to their life?

Which one do you think will have a better outcome?

What do you think their lives will be like?

Imagine as you go through this book.

CHAPTER 3
SEVEN MONTHS AGO – "BEFORE"

I am in Maui as I write this. Sitting inside my little kitchenette with the window open, blowing fresh Hawaii air through my soul.

I was in the midst of selling my house and moving to Mount Shasta just days ago. For three months, my house was on the market and not moving. I dropped the price twice. People walking through my house, having to always keep it clean. Nothing. The contract to buy my house was canceled for "Failure to perform." I was living Groundhog Day. There are no errors. I never question anything. It wasn't time. I still had stories to visit.

Being ocean front in my Newport community, my living and dining rooms face the ocean. My bedroom faces the road. I was looking out my bedroom window in the morning to see the same people, doing the same thing, wearing the same uniforms, every single day. I was on a merry-go-round. I realized that I was on a cycle that had to have something significant change for me to get this storyline back in forward motion. As if I have any say over any of this.

Apparently, what I thought was my absolute next step was not accurate, or I would be elsewhere right now.

As I write this, watching the whitecaps grow with the predicted wind, my house in Oregon is now going to sell. I had to do something radical to break the circle-cycle. I felt it.

I knew I was to go to Maui when I was guided to respond to an email from Alaska Airlines. Living in Oregon, I knew travel by air was not in the cards. I have Alaska miles, but every flight I checked on since I've been here would connect me through Seattle. I would have to stay a night before flying anywhere. The airport is a three-hour drive from my house.

Today everything changed. Alaska flies direct from Portland to Hawaii. That opened me up to immediate action.

I was anti-Hawaii as the only Hawaii in my past was with my ex and his family. My ex was just like his deceased father. They make all of the plans. They know what is best for everyone. You may think you have a say in what your life on vacation will look like, but you realize you never do. When it hit me that this could be perfect, it was having him out of the picture that changed everything. My life has been mine for quite some time now. How did I ever give my power away?

The flight was easy to book. The accommodations were simple, timing out perfectly. I reserved a car, as well as a room for sleep before and after my flights, and parking at an airport motel in Portland. The simplicity of all components falling together made me know this was no different than my trip to Sedona. The same four components were booked. The rest is always up to guidance. I live life with no expectations ever, except for one thing. I always expect miracles. They always deliver.

I am going to get my first book done while I am here. I just know it. This feels so delicious as it is time for the words to be shared. I know once my feet land back on Oregon sand, my life is about to get real, and busy.

For those beautiful souls who have "hitched their star to my wagon" along the way, I thank you. I know I can be radical and harsh, but I speak what I am told. I was harsh and you still didn't hear me. You asked me to yell. You weren't ready.

I am grateful that you looked around and found that I am not the only one who speaks these words. Those of us who speak all know the same information. You get to find the lens you want to filter this message through. This is why there are so many messengers out there. Each one of us has our own expression.

What comes through me, comes through to all of us who are open to receive. I know you want to be like me and walk in bliss every moment of every day. Some of you are so very close, and others have major obstacles ahead. No matter what your path is, stay the course. Do not wander.

Remember to only always take one step. Never look beyond that one step as planning for "the future" will send you on life-altering switchbacks. The only thing that is ahead of you for your pre-planned destiny is one step. Find it. Listen for it. Do not think about next Sunday or your vacation plans for Christmas.

Only one step is to be taken at a time. Planning and thinking stop the steps from coming.

How can you know what that one step is? For those who are truly wanting to walk this walk, I will tell you what you absolutely must do.

You can cry, whine, call your mama, do whatever you want, or simply stop listening to me now. The only thing that will get you from there, to here is

You have to shut up. You have to stop talking to humans. You have to stop needing to be near others. You have to not use your phone. You have to not watch TV. You will argue that you "need" people or your phone, but that is just you needing to remain small. You don't have what it takes to do the work of creating a magical life. I get it. Stay stuck in your little story.

The only way from there, to here, is complete silence. Find a picture or a nature-scape you enjoy and plant yourself there. No phone. No music. Silence. Look. Listen. Be still. Just #STFU.

Walk in nature. Sit by the sea. Look at birds. Watch butterflies. Pull weeds. Plant a garden. Paint a picture. Take a bath. Climb a mountain. Rake a picture in the sand. Build cairns. Fly a kite. Do something that takes your attention so your mind is turned off. Keep your focus on your task. Don't allow thoughts to enter. They will always come back.

For you to find your soul, you have to remember who you are and why you are here. Being ravaged with reality and the sounds of the city is not conducive to activating this part of yourself.

If you want to find your way home, you have to go there first. Get away from everything, and everyone else. Turn all notifications off of your phone. Do not let it ring or show you how much you missed. Like a child or an animal, your phone is an anchor. Trust that this thing is not your friend.

Watch the movie "Her" and try to have a perspective from decades ago. Bring a camera and a recorder to document everything when you go to nature.

Intentionally go where you have no signal if you cannot leave that thing behind.

How long should you be silent? That depends on you.

My last eight years will be documented completely in books. My steps were first to shut up and surrender. I realized my life wasn't working out. I wasn't living happy. I had illness. It meant it was time for me to stop "trying" to make it into something that it wasn't to be. It wasn't working. I was searching and desperate.

I surrendered. I allowed. I threw my paddles in the water and laid back in my boat. After seven years of floating downstream in surrender, I met God. I stopped "doing" anything. I didn't "try" to make anything happen ever again. It was magic. We have much power when we stop trying to be powerful.

When you walk with God, you are never alone. God is truly your right and left hand, and always your best friend. God is fun and has incredible humor. God is light.

Now my "alone" time is never alone. I realized I have never been alone. I have always been good by myself, but now I understand why. Alone is never. I have always been in great company. I have never been lonely.

This is where I ask those who have always had God in their lives. You claim that you are lonely when you are surrounded by so many people. How and why are you lonely? When everywhere you turn, He is right there.

You are lonely because you don't realize that you are not alone. You don't "believe in God." The one you know well, the one you have always loved and prayed to, is not "out there." Your best friend is not helping others in distant countries. We are all sparks of God. God is part of every single one of us.

When you allow God to be the light that shines in your soul and not think of it as something "out there," beyond your reach, it will change you. God is in all of us. God is all of us.

I love walking for miles on the beach and seeing so many people alone – mostly female. We are finding that we can be completely and authentically ourselves when we don't have other people to rely on. When we don't have to compromise; when we can just "be" and do absolutely anything we want, we are complete. Why would we ever want to be somewhere like Hawaii and not follow our own arrow?

That was me. I didn't know how important my own guidance and cravings were to my soul. If we don't feed our soul, who will? No one.

We are here to feed our souls and feel the benefits of breathing in life as we create it. We create our own reality. We are bliss or misery. It is all our choice.

CHAPTER 4
WHO DO I THINK I AM

The woman writing this book is 5'3" and I weigh 112 pounds. To get this material to come through me, I had to find a spiritual path. That miracle began in the fall of 2016. I followed that path relentlessly.

Almost eight years later, I went from a normal operating human (I call NOH in other books), to someone who you call "enlightened." I have reached the highest vibrational potential I can while still walking around on this earth in a skin-bag. I have five other books that have been written and never published. This is for a reason.

If any of the works were published, Cari, the person would not be the same. You have to plug yourself into a brand-new reality when you are a published author. People have questions. You need to speak further about what you have shared. I know this. I knew when I was published my world would never be the same. This book couldn't come through me. I would be plugged in elsewhere.

After I finished writing the fifth book in January, I thought I was done. It is at the publisher's right now being born. After I submitted it, I thought I may be due for a vacation. I know better. In this vibrational space, there are no vacations. There are no "days off."

I represent no one but my own little self with every word I say. I have been removed from your reality for years. I am never around humans. Everything is my take on what I see or experience. I am not influenced by you. You cannot influence me. I don't watch news or TV. I don't hear anything outside of myself except when I listen to music or am out listening to you all complain, whine, and moan about your reality.

I have been removed from being near humans for this very reason. It is energy-depleting when you hear every single soul perpetuating the reality they have created. You hear how horrible it's getting; worse and worse every day. Exactly. Because you believe it is true. Because you see it. Because you manifested every single miserable or beautiful day of your life. If you chose differently, you would see a different result.

I don't see what you see. My world is rainbows and butterflies. Make that Steller's Jay, squirrels, crows, and all kinds of new critters I'm attracting. They are the most beautiful souls on the planet. They keep me lifted. They are what we all are at our core. You should watch them carefully. You have left their universe.

This book that I am to write is only through my lens. The lens that I view everything through. It is painfully honest. I say the things others think but can never say out loud. When I speak, you all agree. But you wonder how I can be bold enough to speak the truth. Do you not see a problem here? This is why I have to write this book. You are all living in fear. No one will say how they feel. You can't speak the truth. Most of you don't even know what it is anymore. You are waiting for instructions.

I never imagined I would dictate a book while crying because of what man has become. This book came through me in two weeks. Other straggler messages came along as well that were to be included. Because I am publishing another book through a publisher and I know how long the process can take, I am zipping through this and publishing on Amazon. After this is submitted, the promise is in eight days this book will be live. It has to be seen. Our lives depend on it.

With what I've witnessed and experienced, I can only share the truth. I have to write this book. Because this is sickening. You are sickening. I am disgusted by what you are doing. I do not agree. I don't watch it. I will not perpetuate it. I am doing the only thing I can do by sitting silently, praying, and holding onto the light. If it wasn't for light workers like me, this planet would be smoke and ash already. We are the only ones holding this planet together. You are not making it easy.

These words haven't been written yet. It's an opinion that has not been stated or seen. This information will be taken seriously. There's so much going on right before you, and you act as if you cannot see it. You are looking at something else because you're distracted. This was not the plan. You are not to be distracted. Put your attention back to front and center; get your needle in your groove. You need to figure out where the heck you are. You are sinking. You are in quicksand, and you don't even know it.

If words come out of my mouth and land in your direction, pay attention to them. My words are not to start a conversation. They are facts. You know it because you grab them like money falling from the sky. I can't know you. How can I know what you need to know? This is why I can't speak to you. If it becomes a conversation, I can't continue on.

I am alone because I can't have conversations. When I say something to you – you always want to sell me the list of reasons why you can't do something. I know better. I know we are unlimited. I cannot continue to listen to you fight for your smallness. This is why I write. I write, and then I hit send and I go. I don't go back. This is why I can't do the rewrite of the first book I wrote. I can't look at that life. I can't even resemble it.

CHAPTER 5

ANSWERING MY CALLING

I have probably written 50,000 pages over the last few years. They're all saved. They're all everywhere. During my transformation from a normal operating human into what I am now, I documented every step along the way. I documented every step before I even knew this was a thing. I have been a historian. A documentarian. Someone who keeps records. Me?

I've known I had some really important words to get out and get published, and I know going to the grave taking powerful stories with us is wrong. We come here to share our experiences. We come here to share what we learned that maybe somebody else doesn't know. It takes a village. We are the village.

We were once a village on this planet. And now we've evolved into something that none of us can begin to recognize. We now have castles in the sky. We have ivory towers. We have penthouses so high up we can't even see them. How did this happen? How did we get to where we are? Where are we?

This is the story I was born to write. Everything that is being published that I've written already comes from so many perspectives. It comes from a panel. It comes from people who have passed on. This book is the culmination of everything I've seen over my life that I know is wrong with our planet. My own eyes have seen this. I have witnessed it. This is part of the reason why I have been chosen to write this story. My eyes have been used for over 60 years. And they have seen the same things you see. I just see it differently than you do. You see it and you're okay with it. I see it, and I'm not. And I don't understand how you can be. You walk right by what is going on acting like it's nothing, and you float by remaining in your little universe, as if your world is perfect.

The first book I'm publishing right now is the most paranormal, woo-woo crazy thing most humans couldn't even imagine. It was not written for the general public. Many of them will read it just to know my dark, dirty secrets; people who want to be a voyeur in my life. But it is very much spiritual in nature.

In order for me to write what I write; I have to be completely without fear. I have seen people who like what I write, people desperately would love to support me and share what I write, but they are too afraid, and they admit it. They know they cannot look at my reality and say it's okay they agree with me. They do agree with me, they just are scared to death to say it in front of anybody. If they do, they will be noticed as somebody who agrees with me.

You are all living in fear, shaking in your shoes at all times. You believe there is a certain way to do things because you were told if you don't do it that way, here's the consequence.

Becoming Immaculate - From Abused to Zen in One Lifetime, will explain beliefs and how they alter the course of your life. In this book, I am talking about this reality only. How we become who we become and how it is not who we are.

In order for me to say the words I say, I can't fear consequences. At any point, I can have somebody with a gun aiming straight at my heart from far away. At some point, they might hate themselves enough to pull the trigger. People want to shut people like me up. But I don't care. I have God on my side. I am fearless. These words have to come out.

This little woman in Mount Shasta is fearless enough to say them. Because you don't scare me. You can't hurt me. I planned this existence and I found my way home. I am still living on this planet, yet I am basically in a skin bag. I exist from heaven. That is why I am writing these stories. You cannot kill me. You can try. The body might drop. But I will never go anywhere.

I am fearlessly writing this book that is going to tell Americans We have really screwed the pooch.

And you continue to screw the pooch. You are the problem.

CHAPTER 6
THROUGH AN ENLIGHTENED LENS

This is critical. This is the book I was born to write. This is the Bridge. I had to write the first five books in order to live the life experience. I wrote until the expansion was complete. After it was complete, I was sent on a cruise.

I realize many things about the writing of this book. Namely, I had to be isolated with no thought of anyone or anything for it to come through as it is. I have had to remain completely isolated and silent. I go where I'm told when I'm told, and then I return home. This book is a lot for me to swallow. It's the truth. It needs to be heard. But as I'm dictating, a chapter or whatever comes through, then I am given a break. It is during those breaks that I realize how powerful what I am saying is. And I am given moments to cry. To melt. To fall apart.

It needs to be said, and nobody is even alluding to it. We act like this isn't real. But this is the truest truth you've seen in a very long time. It's been written in many ways. For so many reasons, you act like what you read is not real. You act like you don't know what you are doing. I am the only one driving this bus, so from my perspective, I can't understand how you can't know.

This is through my very private lens. There's not an ounce of influence from anybody else in this person. It is all my perspective. It is my eyes that have witnessed what my heart took me to. My heart had the experience; my brain is turned off. I didn't have to feel what you are going through.

You all think you're doing the right thing. It's so fun that you look at people like me as hippies. We are always that black sheep of the family that ran away and was just different from the get-go. You're very honest, that's very true. That's what we look like. And I remember very clearly being a little poor girl in my polyester outfits, heading to elementary school, and seeing people who look like me. I thought the same thing too. Gypsies. Whatever was on TV at the time, that was the image I was given. Plus, I had a stepsister in third grade who was a full-fledged flower child/hippie. I was pretty familiar. I am not that image.

Black sheep and hippies. We are just people who don't fit in anywhere. We see what is truly going on. We knew we no longer fit into the cookie-cutter little boxes on the hillside world that we've been living in. When it starts feeling off, you have got to get out. You've got to follow your gut. I was fortunate. I was planning on it. Many just can't take the pressure.

There are all kinds of things we resort to when we can no longer handle pretending to be something we are not. Being the black sheep to me is a grand prize. There is no black sheep in our family. We were all black sheep. But in general, I am a black sheep to the world. And there's no one I would rather be.

I see visions of the chaos you are creating. You are heading as a group toward, yet not looking at something. I'm not seeing it with my human body. I see you're walking straight into the showers. You're walking straight into self-destruction. Voluntarily. You act like you don't even know it. You are doing this by choice. You are choosing your path of destruction that is affecting everyone else on the planet. And you are okay with this. You say I don't see it. Oh, you will. Oh, you will.

I don't watch TV. I haven't seen the news, listened to it, or looked at a headline in years. As soon as I see a story being reported if I have music on or if I'm streaming something. I run to hit mute. Last time I hit mute, I received this download:

I can't see the news from the same perspective that you do. I look at it now and to me it is laughable. I know who we are and why we are here. We do these things intentionally. We come here to be on the news, doing crazy things, reporting crazy stories. Life was so vanilla. We had to make the stories even crazier than they were before. Oh, you've done a grand job

When I have to explain to people how the sexual revolution had to change. When I was young, it was flamboyant; we went through aids in the early 80s. Everything has already been done, so we had to kick it up a notch. We created LGBTQIABCDEF, became non-binary, changed pronouns, etc. We have the awareness that we can be anything we feel, want to be, or nothing at all. I can't wait to see what we come up with next. Everything is cyclical. Everything goes through its cycles of upheaval disease, and magic.

When you're watching these stories, and you get angry at these stupid people for doing stupid things, you are continuing the crazy. If you realize these people came here to do the stupid things they are doing, would you let them off the hook?

What about all of those stupid things in your past? Whether they made the 5:00 news or not, you did them. Most of us are grateful that most of our life is not judged. When you make the news Prepare for a landing. You will be judged.

I see these stories coming and I quickly hit mute. I don't want to hear what upsets you these days. You're coming up with crazier things. I know nothing matters. Nothing matters at all. If you get upset about anything, you are living in and stirring constantly a pot of shit.

From my viewpoint, there is no crime. There is no bad energy going on anywhere. I would not allow that near me. By getting yourself so deeply involved in what is going on. You lower your vibration. You are unplugged from your reality, and you are plugging into something that has nothing to do with you. By doing this, you are slowly killing yourself. The more things that make you sad or angry, the closer you are to the grave. You're not watching nature documentaries that can make you happier, peaceful. You're watching the stuff that makes you mad. That is why, you are killing yourself. The more you get involved, the closer you are to the shovel.

When someone commits a crime and you get to know about it, you throw shade at them and say: what a disgusting and vile being they are. No, they're not. They had an agreement with the person at the other end of the crime to do what they did. Everybody that you've bumped into, in a good or bad way you had agreements with. What they did is not vile or disgusting. They executed a plan. They did exactly what they set out to do. They don't care about the ramifications of the crime; they came to see what those experiences *feel* like.

This is why I look at it from a different perspective. They planned it. They each had to experience what they had to experience. One had to pull the trigger. The other had to die by being shot. We want to experience what it feels like to do these things. That's all in the other book.

You see them as criminals and pigs. I see them as getting through a story. Now, after a crime, what happens next is what is next for them. If they are a victim, their story will go on forever. If they are empowered and strong, they will blast through anything. We are unlimited. All written in the other books.

When you realize this, from where I stand, you don't see things and get angered or upset. They are doing what they came here to do. No different than the experiences you've had in the stories you've walked through. They are just checking boxes that they had to check before they could move into the next lesson they wanted to learn.

Is there any human being on the planet who will argue with me that we get gut instinct? We get tugs from our gut that guide us through our life. Intuition. Am I right or am I wrong? Do you get any form of guidance whatsoever?

Writing this book is stating the obvious. It is clear as can be before my eyes. It's fascinating to me that I am the only one who sees what is going on.

I'm going to try to break this down into the simplest steps.

Where I am in my life now, is beyond magically blissful. My life wasn't working, I was not happy, I had illness, I knew I was supposed to find something else. When I realized that trying it my way wasn't working, I gave up. I didn't give up; meaning I wanted to end my life. I wanted to end a life that wasn't perfect.

I completely surrendered. I didn't have God in my life. There was the universe, my higher power, source I didn't know what to call it. I looked upward with my arms to the sky and said "I give up. I surrender. You take over. I'm not doing a very good job."

What my books are about is how magical life is when you do what I did. It truly is all you need to do. You need to realize that you think you have control, to accept that you don't, and to just shut up and listen. That is how I changed my life. I have four books in a series coming out describing this reality. In the meantime, this is the story I have to write.

For you to understand it, I'm going to explain the guidance as best I can for you to understand. When I surrendered, that meant I stopped trying to make things happen. I stopped planning. I stopped thinking about what I might want to do. When I did that, one step at a time, I was shown what to do. When we try to take two steps or plan what to do next Thursday, we miss the most important step. The one that takes us where we need to go.

This is in my next book, but I will also use it here. This was the chart I was shown to create.

It demonstrates a life of planning and trying to figure things out. It also demonstrates a life of surrender, listening for the next step, and then following it. When I made this change, my path went from switchbacks that would take me around mountains, to slowly, one step at a time, straight up to the top.

I follow guidance. We have gut instinct at all times. You only hear it when you want to. I, now hear it as my only voice. It is who I am. I just follow my higher self and it has taken me where I have arrived. Trusting that you do have a voice within you somewhere that knows better than you, that is where this book is coming from. It's trying to talk to your higher self to remind you who you are and why you are here. No matter if you're the poorest person on the planet, or in the ivory towers in the sky, this is for everyone. You are not being your authentic self. And you know it.

My guidance has become immaculate over the last seven years. Everything in my life has become immaculate. I was brought to the most perfect place to live silently and peacefully with the animals to get these words written. I am here to be a voice of common sense. That seems to be the thing we are lacking desperately in our country right now.

Watching this planet unfold lately, I thought we were dumb and dumber. Then, we became stupid and stupider. Just when you think it can't get any crazier, you do another stupid thing. It gets so much more ridiculous that you look around to see where the camera is. Is this seriously really happening? Are we doing all of this insanity right in front of each other and we're saying it's okay? I swear I am being punked. This is a big trick and it's on me. It can't be real.

Nope. You've gone crazy!

The answers to *why we are the way we are* is in the pages of this book. I suggest you take your time reading it. I suggest you identify who you are in this book. You're going to find yourself in this book. You're going to know exactly when I'm talking to you. It's going to rip your fucking heart out. You're going to see who you are. You're going to hear that you do not have to be who you are. But you are only who you are. How can you possibly be anything else? Because you are not who you are born to be.

You are who you were told you were going to be. There is a big difference.

CHAPTER 7
OUR MISSION ON THIS ROCK

There are many ways to enter this planet. Birth was the first way. Now it's invention, creation, and test tubes; God knows what is going on in labs today. My own child told me she was never born. Okay then. Her removal date was June 24. I never gave birth to anything. Truly. I will never complain. I barely gained any weight. I was barely in maternity clothes.

What happens after that baby leaves the birth canal determines the life of that child. What happens before that child is in the birth canal determines the life of that child. What is the truth?

This is how it works. By the time we are born and being held by Mama, our spirit is locked in the skin bag ready for the ride. Our life plan was already created. We already know where we want to go and what our final destination plan is. For me, I have always known I would be speaking on stage; it just took my entire life to find out what I was to talk about.

We enter into the human reality in order to learn lessons. We come here to master these lessons, to move beyond them, and then to take on new more challenging assignments. We set ourselves up for everything that we are going to go through.

We set up who our parents are going to be. Our siblings, our family. The role models we will stumble across throughout our life. The people who will offer us books. The people who we will bump into will end up being the best accident we ever had. We are going to run into people throughout our lives who we set into place to nudge us back on track when we are lost.

All those magical and serendipitous things that happened throughout your life, the ones that make you shake your head like How did that just happen? You planned it. You have them ready to show up when you need them. It is truly simple.

We said big plans in motion. Death, heartache, loss, tragedy, relationships, affairs, insecurity, psychological issues. You name it We plan some of the craziest stuff you could ever imagine. Since it's all been done before, some of the stories I hear today, continue to blow me away. We are never at a loss of creativity. That is for sure.

We are born to try everything. We come here to be every color of the rainbow; to be every sexual orientation of the rainbow. To be rich, poor, the slave, and the slave owner. We come to do all of it.

The way the universe works is every single one of us comes here with an authentic plan, voice, and arrow. We are pre-calibrated. We know exactly what we want to accomplish and how we want to get there. What we don't calibrate is how the other stories of the other lives we tangle with will stop us in our path. We are intertwined with how they affect our existence. How powerful they are, and how much energy we give them depends on how strong we are.

They are intentionally going to come at you, confuse you, and throw things at you. That looks so much better than Plan B in your stomach. The plan in your gut means you don't need a lot to get through life. It is a very simple plan. But the riches and the gold and the towers of this planet will be enticing. You will be drawn into so many situations that seem so much better than what you came here to do. But you're not totally sure what you came here to do. You just know you have this guidance leading you in a certain direction. You do your best to follow it. When you do follow it, you feel good. You know you are on track. Your needle is in your groove.

But then Larry shows up and offers you that shiny thing, and you could have that shiny thing, plus 20 more, and to get it you need to do this. He makes it sound so easy. Those shiny things are more than you could've ever imagined. You lean into the shiny thing.

Once that shiny thing loses its luster, something else sparkles in front of you and you go that way. Those darn things keep showing up sparkling. They make themselves look so pretty. You cannot help but be led down the road to the sparkly and shiny things.

You feel off. Something isn't right. But look at all the sparkly and shiny things you have. That should feel so good. You figure the more I fight to get more sparkly and shiny things, the better I'll feel.

As you know by now, this doesn't work. You can have all of the gold on the planet, and you can still be the emptiest soul in the universe.

I'm going to explain why.

There is a way to live as a human, and not have icky feelings, ever.

Let's just say if someone was born with no interference whatsoever, they would find their path to their glory quickly. They would find a way to slide their needle directly into their groove, and they could easily follow it every moment of every day. You follow it because when you know it, and step out of it, you know you are off. This is what I do now. But it took me a lifetime to get here.

Once we find our path, once we see how good it feels to be completely in alignment with us, following our arrow, we live in bliss. It merely takes practice. Like everything else. If for some reason you feel out of alignment, like something has shifted and you don't feel as delicious as you did before, you course correct immediately. You know how good it feels to be in alignment, so you immediately get your needle back in the groove, and the record no longer will skip. With practice, you know how to feel good at all times.

When you feel good at all times, you will never have illness again. You will never have sadness. You know how it feels to feel good because you know what to do to get there.

When you listen to only your gut, intuition, or higher self, it will always take you to the exact place you need to be. Unfortunately, we live in a world with distractions. Getting there is harder than being born. Truly. But it is very doable. The only thing you have to do - that is going to be the hardest thing you can ever imagine – is to turn away from everyone in your universe.

Everyone on this planet has plans for you. The only plans that matter ever are the plans you made before you entered the birth canal.

When anybody tells you a direction you should consider going, thank them, and suggest maybe they should go. If anybody wants to use a remote control in your reality, it means they are not dealing with their own. That would be everybody on the planet.

Giving anybody power over your reality is the first big no-no. If anybody inserts their reality or preplans your existence in any way, you are automatically starting off on the wrong foot. Doesn't that sound horrid? It is. You have more to undo than I did.

In this book, I'm going to explain how this world can be the most magical planet in the stratosphere. We have gotten so off track; it will be shocking if we can find our way back during our lifetimes. I do know it is possible. I hope these books are found and eventually, they will turn this planet around. But I do know we can do it quickly.

Thought - thoughts in your head are all we need to change this planet.

How you think creates your reality.

When you think the same as thousands of other people, you create a reality together. Good, bad, and indifferent.

I have not seen the news in years. When I was on the radio, I had to glance at headlines to have an idea of what was happening. Even then I barely looked. Looking at what is going on destroys your insides. It gets your emotions churning and burning. It makes you angry. It makes you sad. You feel _____ all of the people who are _____.

The anger and hostility you feel towards countries, people, entities, anything, it eats you up and becomes a cancer inside. Why are you angry? What have they done to you?

I'm going to try not to go too deep down any avenue, but the collective consciousness on the planet is what is causing the turmoil on the planet. I don't know what your headlines are today, but it is always ugly. You don't want to speak to anyone who has good things to say because you need to stay mad. You want to drive your point home. It feels like everyone is ready to give up on us. It looks like we've completely given up on ourselves.

I hope this book hits an audience that I don't think people are expecting me to hit. My target audience for this book is the privileged. The children who live in ivory towers. The children who were born as utility items because they are not allowed to have their own reality. They are part of a company, or corporation, a reality that is pre-ordained, and they will have their part to play.

CHAPTER 8
TAKE ME TO YOUR LEADER

No matter where you are in the world if a spaceship or 300' tall Sasquatch-looking critter came into your land today and said to you, "Take me to your leader." Where would you take them? Give it a minute. Think about it. You can't come up with one, can you?

Exactly my point.

When I was young, the head of the household was the man in charge. You could see it on every television show. Dad was the dude, the man. "Wait till your dad gets home" sound familiar? The strong and respected person beyond dad would be the President of the United States. We knew the man leading our country could be trusted with our lives and the lives of our children. We had stock in being a creator in this land of the free.

I didn't, but many kids grew up with priests, preachers, or clergy. I know this layer was a safe space where you could go for answers if you couldn't find them in the walls of your home. We all knew there was always someone who had the answers. Today, who would you say is our leader?

If you are in England, do you choose the Prime Minister or the royal family? Who would be the first "human" to come to mind if someone asked for your leader? Think about it. If you had to pick, who is it? Who would you trust with the lives of your kids and animals?

We will go much deeper into this subject.

I would like to personally thank Donald Trump for doing the one thing he did well. He dismantled the foundation that formed the respect for our country, the United States. His ridiculous and very childlike behaviors showed the world that everything we thought was solid, powerful and ours, was merely all built on shifting sand.

I couldn't believe this story was unfolding right before our eyes on the news. The "party" stood behind him and allowed him to disrupt the consistency of our country. We all said it was okay to behave as such and run for "the most powerful position in the land." I kept feeling like it was all a big joke and at any moment, we would all be let in on it. What respectable president would be behind such a topic as "pussy-gate!" I bet Bill Clinton was relieved when this man stepped forward. We all know George Jr. was every time The Donald opened his mouth.

I watched his TV shows. This man loves to tear people down and rip them apart. He is after all the self-appointed authority. On what? I have no idea. I was amazed watching someone who was so full of himself; and the next thing you know, you think he is a smart choice to run our country. Have you seen the inside of his house or his life?

Clearly, nothing has meaning. Nothing is solid. After all, nothing is real. Thank God I understand this.

The year of the election between Hillary and Donald was the year everything in our world went to hell. I know we all had to feel like we were being punked when a man who had a television show about firing people would be considered to lead our land. He, and the wife of a previous president.

Watching the election unfold was a joke. He demanded Obama provide proof of citizenship when he was a mere civilian. Running for president, he said "no" anytime he felt like it. His constant vile treatment of women and humans was all I could ever see of this man. I never had a clue what his political ideas were for running the country. I couldn't get beyond his disgusting character. I knew America was too great of a country to allow such a debacle to unfold. This could not be happening. How can it be down to these are our only two choices? Well, because we agree to it.

I remember my ex sitting on the edge of the coffee table that night as the results were slowly coming in. The next day we would either have Hillary Clinton as our first female president, or Donald Trump as the biggest joke this country had to put on a ballot. All I knew was the damage was already done. The entire campaign and mudslinging dismantled our universe. There was no turning back now.

We couldn't unring this bell. It rang loud and long across all the land. No one missed the show. By now, it didn't even matter who was elected. We showed our colors. We showed we were flawed and we had cracks in our system. We showed the world that we are not as strong and powerful as we all thought we were. We had two people representing the only system you believe can work in America.

Enough of you are so confused about politics that you can't wrap your head around what is going on. You want to get involved, but you don't want to appear clueless. Believe me, we are all clueless. Politicians are confused. Enough of you can easily change an election if you understand what you need to do. I promise your machine will rally. Keep your eyes open.

Why do we keep using a machine that has clearly shown it cannot work any longer? When the two candidates that our life depends on are both bad choices, where does that leave us? Before this, I believe we had enough strength and respect to trust that "all was good in the world." That ended with the beginning of that election that was fatal for our country.

There are so many good choices out there. Listen to those who speak their truth and they back it up with history and their personal life. We can't know what is going on behind these machines. The man out front is merely a talking head. The machine controls the choices. Follow the money. Candidates today cannot follow a personal path. It is not about personal desire and passion to help our country. They are the driver of a very big and powerful bus. The bus has dark-tinted windows. You cannot see who is on the bus but they can see you. Believe me, they know who you are. They know everything about you.

I went to bed early as I knew it was over. It didn't matter what happened next. The year of mud-slinging, story creation, and bad press for all was just the beginning. The election may be over tomorrow, but we are already the laughingstock of the planet. At least it is over. It was just the beginning.

We can no longer be transparent. The Donald showed the world that there are no rules, and he will happily break every one of them. And y'all said it is okay. And you are still saying it's okay. It is not okay. You sitting quietly while your world falls apart is in your hands.

Did you see where I said the majority of us are confused? A majority can change anything. Positive and uplifting beliefs and thoughts can destroy any machine driven by darkness, secrets, power, or money. Trust that we have enough within us to bring this country back to the respectable and powerful land we once knew we were.

The system doesn't care about you. You are confused. Let's change the system!

CHAPTER 9
BOPA

My grandfather was a very wise man. As a matter of fact, looking back at my childhood I believe he was the only wise man I knew. We were very close. He shared things with me that he couldn't share with others. He knew I got it.

My grandfather raised three boys and one princess. I loved all of my uncles. They were the highlight of my childhood. We didn't have a lot to look forward to.

My grandpa had a bad heart. He had all kinds of health issues. But he was a trooper. He kept trooping and plugging away.

He didn't realize he created a monster in how he raised my grandmother until it was time to do something about it. Her only responsibility was taking care of my mother, Princess Ginger. He would take care of everything else. And he did.

Grandma became the beck-and-call girl anytime my mother had a problem or was about to do something stupid. The day my mom shot my dad, I had to call Grandma. She always came to the rescue.

Grandpa realized if he wanted to cross over, she would flail without him. She didn't know how to do anything. So, he had a goal. He was going to leave the hospital after his second to last trip. Over the next six months, he would train Grandma how to pay bills, how to write checks, and how to put gas in the car. She knew nothing. He did everything.

I was visiting him in the hospital from Ohio when he made this declaration. He had to train her so he could leave with a clear conscience. He was tired. His body was done. After the conversation, I flew back to Ohio.

Around six months later I got the call that Grandpa was back in the hospital. I went. I was with him alone in his room when everyone else in the family was in the waiting room. They were pacing. They were frantic. He had to get better. They all told him how critical it was that he bounced back. *Come on Grandpa, you've only had a few strokes and heart attacks. What's wrong with you?* He had quadruple bypass surgery, he was tired. He worked his entire life. He wanted to go home.

While I was with him and he shared the pleas from the rest of the family, I gave him a kiss on the forehead. I told Grandpa that he was released and free to exit his body. I gave him permission to go home. Sometimes all it takes is one other to love us enough to let us go.

He could not fix what was out there. It was its own story that would unfold on its own. That could no longer be his problem.

During one of our many profound conversations, he shared many a story about how things were back then. He told me often, "Cari, Man is ruining his own nest."

CHAPTER 10
SIMPLER TIMES

Things that made me happy when I was a child were the simple things. Just like life today. I did not need anything fancy. Being the first one to open the cereal box to get the toy inside was a treat when you had two older sisters. Cracker Jacks; you are guaranteed a special surprise. Life was horrific and tragic, but it was simple. It was our normal.

Looking back, I see the tragedy. But it wasn't tragedy. It was the story I came here to live. But looking back at it as a normal human, it looks sad, disgusting, and pathetically horrible. The pain these children must've suffered. No, these children signed up to suffer. The dads signed up to do what they did. It was all an agreement. Having a horrible life gives you a wonderful life if you choose it. You can become what you are here to be. You can know that you will never go through that experience again. We have choices. Free will to get us to our next story. Free will also keeps us stuck in an old one.

We were poor. It was beautiful. We got to make dollhouses out of cardboard, glue, tape, and string. We made paper dolls out of cardboard and magazine models. We cut out clothes from other models to adorn our paper Barbie's. How many kids today can do this? We were engineers in our early years. We had to be. We had to learn how to make things happen if we wanted anything to happen. We were poor. Poor was normal. We watched our car get repossessed. We went hungry. We ate our pet rabbits. I wouldn't have wanted anything other than the childhood from hell I had. Without it, I wouldn't be here.

The best memories of my childhood were made outside. The standard and daily instruction was, "Go outside and play. Be home when the street lights come on." And we did. It's amazing the things we survived. But we are here to survive. We have a plan. When we go outside and play, we use our imagination. We invent all kinds of games. We role-play. We demonstrate behaviors; either what is going on in our house, or what we want to be going on in our life. Pretending was the only way to get from where we were, to places we could only dream of.

I remember all the girls playing house at recess in sixth grade. It confused me very much. They were playing happy roles as mothers with babies. I couldn't understand how they could play house when 'house' was so ugly inside. It was all I knew. I looked at them with wonderment.

The world I grew up in was very simple. I lived in Henderson, and Las Vegas, Nevada for the most part. I moved 26 times by the time I started sixth grade. I did see a little bit of the world in my childhood. What I saw was that we were very much equal.

In the Las Vegas Valley, Nothing looked extraordinary other than the hotels and the nightlife. The houses looked alike. The people dressed alike. We did our hair the same. There were different kinds of clothing, nothing that stood out as something extremely expensive or designer. We had labels, but everything was simple. Nothing was extravagant or extraordinary. Everything was average.

Although my family life was in no way healthy or wealthy, the world seemed pretty simple and easy. No one seemed special. Everybody seemed to fight for the same causes. Everybody knew what was right and what was wrong. We weren't censored. We had opinions. We hurt feelings. We also got over it. We all had to. That's called living. It's called life. We don't live in a bubble. We don't live in a vacuum. We live in a world full of all kinds of good and icky stuff. We have to adapt. That is just what life is, or what it was "back in the day."

You didn't feel division in your friends or neighbors. The different income levels were all mixed in with the rest of the folks. Around the corner from where I worked on Tropicana was Liberace's house. It was fun to walk by and see the beautiful piano and all the mirrors from his wide-open front window. Driving down Sunset Road, you went by Wayne Newton's house, "Casa de Shenandoah" is the name of the property.

You expected him to have a big piece of property, he was a big thing in Las Vegas. His job was performing and entertaining, so he needed a tall fence. If not, he would be swarmed. But nothing stood out. Nothing separated us back then. Everybody had "a job" or "a career path."

You made a certain amount of money with your job, and you were able to pay bills. There were no extreme salaries. Everything had a bracket. Everything was attainable. It was pretty transparent. We got to step into our lives with awareness and figure out who we were going to be. We also got to flail and flop and flounder. Our lives were right before us. They were in our hands.

Many of us had the opportunity to go to college. Many had the requirement that they were going to college. Many of us didn't even know there was an option like college. It wasn't a language spoken in my house. We never saw it as an option. We didn't have family with higher education. We had a lot of stagehands.

The extremely challenging childhood I experienced is why I am where I am. The pendulum can swing as far as we allow it. By living the crappiest childhood, I'm having the most delicious adult life ever. I found the path to the fifth dimension, and I wrote a book about it. That is where I live full-time.

After being silent, and not speaking to anyone but an occasional neighbor conversation, my waiter, or the people at the store, I'm completely silent. I don't talk on the phone. When and if I communicate now, it is only via text, Messenger, or email. I cannot do anything live. And some things I just can't respond to. Ever.

By taking this path, I became an empty flash drive. A completely clean slate.

When I was a kid, life was tragic, but it was simple at the same time. We didn't have much so creativity was what we used. I am so grateful for the horrible childhood I lived to talk about. If I didn't have it, I don't know what I would be doing right now.

What I *do* know because I know me, is I would be very unsettled. I almost ended up in multiple parallel directions, but I knew better. I listened to my gut. I would have died long, long ago. I would have taken my life (three suicide near-misses) or died of some dreadful disease. That is what happens when you are not who you came here to be. It gets so bad that one way or another, we find a way out.

CHAPTER 11
LIVING IN SEARCH MODE

In the fall of 2016, the reality that I called 'my life' changed forever.

For all five decades of my life, I was in search mode. I was searching for something that I couldn't see. I found it that fall. My life would never be the same. I was looking for answers, and they showed up. Once that door opened, it was like opening an airplane door in flight. I could not escape the reality I would step into. It was like being pulled into a new world, like a vacuum. But I surrendered. I went freely. And what I learned will astonish you.

We think we know why we are here. We do not. We are doing it wrong. How can I know? What makes me different? I did what you cannot nor will not do. I became silent. I stepped away from people. I didn't like how I felt being around people and the disparity was growing. I realized I became what we came here to this planet to become. I was able to see the difference between what was happening to me, and how unlike everyone else I was becoming.

For the last few years, I was transitioning from marriage and living in Washington to a space where I could be silent. Even when I was still in the house with my ex, I was silent. I have been silent and alone. Imagine twenty-four hours a day never having a conversation with another human. Day in and day out. You would never believe it is something you begin to require. I look at my fire and the mountain silently, and answers come through me.

When we are not outwardly speaking to people, arguing for our limitations, or paying attention to everything icky going on in the world, we find a space of peace and tranquility. It is always there; you are simply choosing to dive deeply into a world of turmoil. Going there, you keep it in turmoil. Not going there, not giving it your attention, it would not exist.

As a race, humans, we are lost. You think you are heading in the right direction, but you are not. You are racing us back toward an experiment that we tried and already failed once before. We are trying to be as technically advanced as we can, not having a clue what the cost is to human life. We are working hard as humans, to replace humans. Can you wrap your brain around this? At the same time, we have programmed our humans to be what we "need" them to be.

Am I really the only one who believes we are being punked by a universe greater than ours? Why would we continue down a path that can't work? Has anyone heard of Atlantis and Lemuria? There was a time when we out-technologied ourselves to destruction. We are on this path again. This time, it is not just technology that is the problem. It is a different kind of programming that is the problem.

Why would we want to replace a human with something that is not human? Humans are the only "thinking" things on this planet. In this book, you will see it is our "thinking," our thoughts that are destroying us. And you clearly have no idea. God, I certainly hope you don't.

CHAPTER 12
CODDLED/ SENSITIVE KIDS

I was the third person standing in line at the grocery store. The tall man approached the tiny cashier lady. His voice could be heard throughout the store as he began yelling at her. My programming took me immediately into my fight or flight mode. My stomach hurt instantly. I was that little girl under my bed longing for the sounds to stop.

When I was young, you had to have thick skin. You had to have a layer of toughness somewhere inside of you to protect you when, and if needed. It was needed often.

I remember lying underneath my bed when voices got loud in the house. The norm was loud voices, then screaming, and then, the furniture would begin to fly. Then the slapping and punching would begin. Under my bed was a haven. For some reason, I felt safe there.

Has anyone but me noticed that we have lost that edge? The younger generations have learned that it is not okay to have thick skin. We need to be vulnerable to our edges and allow anything that anyone says or does to affect us. Why and when did we decide it was okay to give our power away?

During an informational conversation with someone once, they explained the pronouns they require. They also said that when people don't respect them enough to address them properly, it crushes them.

I wanted to spell this out for them. I said, "If they don't call you or refer to you by the pronouns you have requested, then your feelings are hurt when they don't use them, correct?" They smiled as if I finally got it, and confirmed the answer was yes. I then carefully and slowly said, "You do realize that by arming them with this information, you just gave them all of your power, right? If they don't use the pronoun, they can affect how you feel." The look on their face was priceless.

If I don't refer to you by the label you have put upon yourself, you will be injured somewhere deep within wow. This is truly the strangest shift of power I have ever witnessed. Here's how I was not raised, but the conclusion I came to on my own.

The weaker I appear, the weaker I am. If I live by the mantra, "Sticks and stones may break my bones, but names will never hurt me," then no matter what anyone calls me, or says, anything it is up to *me* how I react. When you arm them with your weakness; a method of knocking you down, they will use it.

My suggestion is to stop creating new labels and expectations that we must remember for each living being before us. How about you do you, and I will do me? I won't have any expectations of you, and you have none for me. I will be the best I can be; you be the best you can be. Sound good?

Labels are the wrong answer. Telling someone how they must 'behave in your presence' to not hurt you is insanity. This is a department where we really needn't spend our time. Let's just be who we are and not care what any other living being thinks about us. Okay? Doesn't this sound a little easier? We have big fish to fry all over the world and we are dealing with not hurting people who have decided to become sensitive to words. This is language. We need to get over it.

When my child was young, she competed in baseball, soccer, basketball, and volleyball, and I'm sure something else I'm missing. When they were little, they took score. When she went to junior high school, in seventh grade, it didn't happen. Everyone makes the team. In seventh grade, they didn't keep score. What? By now, most of these kids have competed. Now you are telling them that you are all the same and everyone gets a trophy. This is exactly what went down.

I remember Brad's mom telling him at my kid's baseball game to stay away from the field. On the field was dirt. She taught him early on that dirt was icky. Stay away from dirt. He was in his early two digits, but he already knew that dirt was not to be his friend.

I remember watching shows about the days of pioneers. The land of the free, where you live, did not get here by sensitive Sally. How did we go from being hard-working members of society to allowing a generation of couch surfers to be paid to do nothing?

It is as if we are pleading with a huge sector of the young generation to stay away from becoming a functioning member of society. We are paying them to not do anything. Meanwhile, companies need to hire thousands of young people at an entry-level wage, but American kids are not interested in the job. Help must be found elsewhere.

We have very rich children who attend the best schools, academies, and boarding houses. They receive the degree that is necessary from the proper university to carry on their designated role in the family function. Who they are and what they bring to the party matters not. They are part of something they believe is their life sentence.

Now we have an entire generation of coddled kids. We have decided that being incredibly sensitive is much more important than strength, self-respect, motivation, drive, or integrity. I look at what is going on from my window and you have gone nuts.

A child growing up with everything being done for them, or handed to them, cannot know how to function or be self-reliant. Once that word came through me, everything made sense. Parents now want to have a bigger stake in the lives of their children. I know a few that are living their best dream. Having their kids never leave home was a dream for one family.

When they were young, the dad would often joke that his kids would have to have a place for them when they were old. They were setting their kids up for a future with a parent in the mother-in-law suite. Who wants to have that hanging over them? What if your life takes you to the equator and mommy hates the sun? It turns out that these kids have the option to live in the family home forever. Even with their chosen partners. I'm sure they would build a third floor if grandbabies were coming. This mom and dad are the happiest on the planet. The kids will never be able to find the part of them to access their arrows. They are stuck in the story of the mother.

I made it clear to my kid early on and kept telling her to make sure she heard me, that being taken care of in my "old age" is my responsibility. If I don't set the plans in motion to make sure I have what I need when I'm 120, to not ever take it on as her responsibility. To not allow herself to take on guilt. Others will tell her she should. I am putting it in writing.

I am to take care of myself. My job raising a child was to give the best parts of myself, then kick her out of the nest. Let's just say that I kicked her out with a double-leg punch. Unfortunately, her dad was there to catch her.

This new sensitive generation takes away everything that made this country strong. We are raising weak and entitled children. First, the entitled were those born into it. Now even the middle class and below are creating a generation of kids who are not asked to do anything. They are sensitive because we have allowed it. They are weak and lazy. They will never find motivation or fire in their belly because they have never been shown how to access it. The older they are, the harder it will be. What happens to your child if you drop dead? How will they function?

One of my kids' college friends called off work one day. She was an emotional nightmare. She told them she would be taking the day off for mental health. And it was allowed. This brought tears of laughter to my eyes. What world exists where someone is having a bad day and can simply not go to work because of it? How many people have you stood before in their paid occupation and they were dealing with something horrible? You can't even believe they came to work with their situation. They believe it is the right thing to do. I know people who have never missed a day of school, or a day of work. Yes, many of you are superstars and are doing things for crazy reasons. Many of you just know that you need to be strong to survive in this reality. Allowing something like mental health days opens up another bag we cannot seal. It happened. Step into today. That was yesterday. Let it go.

You have created a generation of couch potatoes who are waiting for the right opportunity that will motivate them to get off the couch. Sadly, when you have no motivation, you will never have motivation.

The only thing that can save these kids is A.) Cutting them off. Kicking them off of the couch and out the door, or B.) Mirror what accomplishment looks like. Lead by example. In the process, however, you have to set them free. They will figure it out. You keeping them as your special little pet does nothing for their reality. If you drop dead tomorrow, who will allow them to continue to function in this capacity? Not one living soul. You have set this kid up for major failure. They will not know how to function when you do it all for them. How can you expect them to know how to do anything when you do it all?

Now we have a generation of "Influencers" teaching us how to screw in lightbulbs. Little do they realize that everything they are teaching us, we learned before we were ten.

To the parents of these coddled kids. What did you think would happen?

His son was 15 ½ and had never heard the word "no" come out of his dad's mouth. That moment when he said "no," we both were stunned. What was the result? While sleeping, the boy took a butcher knife to the kitchen and destroyed it. The cabinets and counters were stabbed to death.

Fast forward, the dad went to two Tough Love meetings with me in hopes of helping his child. The dad could only do two meetings. It was too hard. The thought of having his child not love him for even a moment was more than the dad could take. Rather than go to the meetings that would be a "hard thing" for the dad to do, he did nothing.

Now for doing nothing, his little boy is spending twenty-eight years in federal prison for rape and kidnapping. Sometimes, a little Tough Love and a short lack of love goes a long, long way.

Coddled kids won't work. They don't have to. There are so many opportunities for those who want to work. I have met many young people who have impressed me where I live. Every trade is available for them to step into. They can learn any skill they want. They are needed everywhere.

And then there's coddled kids. They don't know how to do anything. They don't have a skill. They have a degree. They're trying to get a job. Or not. They don't have to.

Because we have so many privileged people on the planet, when a cashier sees you coming, she almost pees herself. If she doesn't smile and kiss your ass, one little click of a survey can destroy her life. And you've done it over and over again. You've assumed the expectation that you needed to be treated like the royalty you feel like you are. Because of the way you are dressed. The way you carry yourself. You need a certain level of respect from somebody behind the counter. This is how you were raised. You believe this.

Believe me, they do too. Because they know if they don't smile, and act like the monkey you need them to be, they can lose their job. This is why I do every survey that I can. These people are scared because they are always on the verge of unemployment. Their perfection is your goal. They are not allowed to have a bad day. They are not allowed to be sad because grandma died this morning and there was no one to fill in their shift. You don't know anyone's story. We don't know yours. The difference is, we don't want to know your story. We just want you to treat us with respect. You are not better than us

CHAPTER 13
THEY WANT TO WORK. YOU MAKE IT HELL

They have to be kind, apologetic, and constantly stroke us to make sure that we are as happy as we possibly can while they are on the phone with us or standing before us. We have become so entitled and demanding of our expectations that if she isn't kissing my ass to make me happy, I can get her fired. That's what people do. I hate people. I hate what we have become. When they squeamishly look at you and say, "There's a survey on the receipt, please take it if you can." They hope to God you are having a good day.

It is hard for those of us who actually want or have to go to work. You make it almost impossible. Because your life is so miserable, you are searching for people to take down and destroy. I pity anyone who stands in your way.

When I started working, I never stopped. Who I was, came through in my work. Customer service was definitely my strong suit. I never dropped the ball. I get answers. I like to solve problems. I like to solve mysteries. Obviously.

I can't understand how anybody can only do something halfway.

Employees now are shaking in their shoes because they are being double-checked and triple checked. They are being secret shopped. They feel that they can't be trusted to do their job when they know they can. They are being secretly and overtly verified. They live in fear because they don't know who is going to be the person who is actually judging them or deciding if they should stay or if they should go. It is a sad world that we have become.

We used to work hard because the work was there and it had to be done. Yes, we deserved a break, but we don't need to give an entire generation a break. To them working hard means we have to be aware of our sensitivities going in. We are emotional and sensitive. We need mental health days. We need stress release. We are an emotional mess. How about I am strong, I am resilient. We are making ourselves disgustingly weak and feminine. Let's get strong and masculine. Let's stand up for ourselves and be who we are. We don't need to be coddled and handheld to do anything. How did we get so soft?

Employees in the customer service field now are scared to death. They are sending surveys to every single human being on the planet that was in front of you. The people who are angry at everybody, and the Susie Sunshine's. These people affect your job based on how they feel when they are in your presence.

We have lost our ability to respect each other and expect a good job and good service. With this recipe, in turn, you have a happy and kind customer. We are now scaring people to death so they don't want to be involved in customer service.

The concierge in charge of my book at Balboa was on leave. I sent email after email and he never responded. After not hearing back, I emailed someone else I had an address of, who was above him. He kept sending me the stock answers that they were all taught how to say. Finally, after I whined enough, he copied yet another person on the emails. Assumably higher than him.

When my guy responded finally, he apologized profusely. He was in trouble on that end, but why? I found out he was on leave. Something happened in his life and he had to be away from work. Why would they not just tell me? I immediately didn't care. I just didn't know why my book cover was horrendous and it took them five minutes to get it done, and now a month later, I'm not seeing a revised cover.

We need to get back to speaking the truth. When people treat us like shit, we do not have to take it. We need to be able to say something to disarm them. Just run them through the checkout, don't make eye contact. Serve them the food, do whatever you need to do Do not smile. You already know they aren't giving you a tip.

As they leave your space forever, in your sweetest voice, utter these words *"Have the day you deserve."* Because they know you mean it.

CHAPTER 14
LOVE. MARRIAGE.
RELATIONSHIPS.

Marriage is a creation of man. It was about land, money, and keeping stuff in the family. God has nothing to do with marriage. Never would God ever want you to make a promise about anything, let alone swearing on your life that you will be with this person until one of you croaks. That certainly sounds romantic and all, but from my lens and knowing how good it feels to always be alone, I beg to differ.

Man invented this legally binding contract. We went so far as to make it something we can hold on to and against each other for the rest of our lives. We get so locked into this family situation that we can almost never leave. We do, but dear lord it has been made daunting. Especially because we are no longer simple people. We have stuff now. We have a lot of stuff. So much that we need to store most of it near the highway.

You have to really hit rock bottom in your relationship to pull the plug on it today. Because I came from blue-collar roots and a poor childhood, leaving a life of comfort, money, travel, ease, play and anything I imagined was hard. But I had to do it. Having a blue-collar background and roots was all I needed for a simple transition.

I remember how good it feels to be simple and to have nothing. I love how it feels to know there is absolutely nothing I want. I walk through stores just to see if something will jump out at me, but it never does. If I "need" something, I get it. I had to walk through the entire Yreka Walmart yesterday just to find electrical tape. I knew approximately where it would be, but I don't know this store. I move fast. I get in and get out.

Being simple takes things that some think are chores and turns them into fun, keeping you strong and warm. They are the things I love doing. I can't chop rounds, but I love hauling and stacking wood. It is something I've done for six months now. I've thrown four cords of wood, two with help.

Doing the simple tasks that you must do to "live" where you live has always been special to me. You can't find your way to your simplest space when you are tangled up in love.

Like our mother, my sister Donna was married five times. After husband number four and child number two, we aligned perfectly for her to change her reality. I was leaving an apartment, and she was leaving her husband. She had a friend with a rental house with a fenced yard that worked perfectly. The place felt wonderful. She had two boys and it had a great yard.

Since her senior year of high school marriage, like our mother, she was never without a husband. After number four, and two kids in tow, she knew she needed to take a break. We moved in together signing a year lease on the house. It was a commitment. We signed on the dotted line. We were going to be there for each other. I would help her break her man-addiction. She had two kids to take care of. They needed their mother.

I will jump to what I found out later. I was being duped. The story was "They met where she took her car in for repair last week." The fact was he was showing up at the bar where she was working for a long time. She was already planning her escape not even three months in.

Why do you believe you must have someone in order to function? My sister had a miserable life and went downhill after she broke our contract. She had to figure it out with her friend and our lease. He could pay for it. I didn't care. I was out.

We think we are stuck with this human for the rest of our lives. And then in church, we were told this sanction was for eternity. You need to lock and load for the rest of your life. Over generations it just became normal. It is just what you do. You get your education so you're all kinds of smart, and then you find that partner. You reproduce, rinse, and repeat. That is not how it is done. We have lost the way. Once we're locked in, we feel stuck so our life is over.

We are stuck in our beliefs and what we've been told our entire lives. We believe that when we find the partner they are to be forever. It has to be an agreement going in. You honestly believe at a very young age that you can commit to this contract and hold it strong. We keep this in mind as we "search" for this person early in life. They have to show up, "Mom had me when she was 16, 21, 17" however young mom was. You "see what has been done before" and you think this is your story. But it is not. This book is to take you back to what we've forgotten. Life is not about partnering up.

Life on this planet is about finding who you are early on and following the arrow down your path until you find your destination. Without getting in your way, you will. When you get there, you meet others who are there. This is when the partner you desire will show up. They will be right where you want and need them to be. They will already be in your vibrational space.

I met who I "believed" was my soul mate when I was nineteen or twenty. I was marrying him. I knew it would be for life.

He has been a dear friend and an active player in my life for over four decades. It is because I left him at the altar. We never would have made it. This is our story.

When I met John O. on the Safeguard Business Systems ski bus to Whistler, I knew it was all over. He was cute, charming, adorable, and so much fun. His personality was something I wasn't used to. He had a brilliant air of confidence. How could I have known that in the back of the bus, very insecure John C. was stewing as I didn't want to marry him at 20 years old. We dated twice.

When we pulled into the parking lot after the trip, two men were in a ring fighting for me. This was a once in a lifetime. Poor John O. didn't see it coming. It didn't last, but it was memorable.

I loved him dearly. We had fun for about a year and a half in southern California. We played crazy dress-up with another couple (our roommates) and walked up and down the Sunset Strip. It was a wild experience. We met so many characters by becoming them. It was beautiful.

John also liked to pretend that we were rich. When I met his parents, we took a limousine to LAX to fly out. When a black stretch limo pulled up to our apartment in Alhambra, I'm sure our neighbors were amused.

I wore a black and white striped dress with a hat. I had a cigarette extender to make me look cool. Or whatever we did that for. Of course, my man went all Gentlemen's Quarterly for the ride.

On the way to the airport, we had a flat tire in the back. The driver was a beautiful and thin woman wearing a tux. This bothered me. We weren't even asked to get out of the car to make it easier. I wanted to help her. He didn't even think about it. It wasn't something that touched his soul as it did mine. I couldn't get it.

She changed the tire and we were off.

When we were picked up at LAX to go home, apparently the wires crossed. Our stretch limo had about twenty seats. We weren't alone.

We moved to Boston together and both quickly were hired again at the New England branch of Safeguard in Newton Center.

Something was off. We had so much fun in LA, and now our wedding was in the next six months. What was going on inside of me?

I loved him with every fiber of my being. He was handsome, the most fun person on the planet, and I know he loved me. I was even becoming a catholic for him so we could get married in his church. He would at least have the wedding of his dreams. I didn't have any dreams of a wedding. With my mother's five husbands (by sixth grade for me) and my sister's five, husbands were like dating to my family. It wasn't special.

I called my sister and asked her to fly to Boston. I was going to leave. I couldn't do this. What in the hell was wrong with me? I saw a life with him. It would be fun and magical. I had to leave.

When I knew she was on the way, I told him in April that I had to have a break. I had to open my head to see what was happening inside. I know the words were loving, yet defensive and pathetic at the time, but my "gut" was totally twisted in knots for weeks. I didn't know what I was being told, I just knew I was creating a cancer if I didn't listen to the feeling.

I broke his heart and rocked his perfect world. When I saw him look at my finger, I pointed to the nightstand. The "full carat marquis, on a Tiffany setting," was on my nightstand. The one he screamed that he sold his stocks and bonds to buy.

Why? I was embarrassed by such a rock. I didn't want it. I only wanted him.

Donna came, and we drove from Boston to Las Vegas. We had a blast. It was great to see her. She had a break from work and the husband had the kid. We made great company.

Once I left, my gut was in complete alignment. Meaning, that all of the icky feelings I had that led me up to leaving – were gone. Completely. I didn't know it then, but when your needle is back in your groove, it feels delicious. I loved him and wanted to be with him. I could not understand this feeling I had for the last weeks prior to my leaving. He was my everything.

It was late April when I left. I knew he would be back in Pennsylvania with his family nursing his wounds on the weekend of our wedding. I flew to Boston on Labor Day weekend to get what I could.

I got a "drive away" service for a car. Someone who moved across the country left a car and needed it delivered. I signed up to take it to LA. I just had to cover gas. It was a big Country Squire station wagon with wood paneling. They had some stuff in it, but there was plenty of room.

Unfortunately, the man who picked me up at the airport had a very small car. I had to get what I could fit in a tiny four-seater with two people before he took me to my ride.

I grabbed my custom-made wedding dress. I forgot the veil. I couldn't fit my sewing machine as it was in a big cabinet. I made us all kinds of clothes back then; I made him a button-down shirt, and dresses for me.

I got what I could, then I high-tailed it out of Boston for good. He didn't know I was there until he returned. It was hard.

He wanted my wedding dress back. He had a huge hand in the creation as again, nothing mattered to me. He loved seed pearls and a certain type of lace. We ended up having the top done by a certain designer and the explosive bottom by another. It was stunning.

I couldn't understand the world he lived in. He wanted the dress back to have it embalmed. He had the veil.

We were going to have a "Cinderella wedding" with all of the trimmings. While we were still in California, he was guiding his mother and brother in Pennsylvania as boots on the ground to get our wedding planned. They had the venue, church, band, and hall for our reception. They had a huge guest list. I guess we had a lot of people coming that I never met. Also covered was our two-week vacation to Paradise Island in the Bahamas. My family couldn't afford to come. I couldn't cover a dime, but I was barely going to have an imprint on this event. I would be Barbie.

I could play this part with no problem. I was going with the flow. I just knew this was not to be my story.

His family and religion were everything. I knew for John O; marriage was for life. It mattered to him. What a long shot I would be with my family history. He never questioned it. I would never do something to hurt someone – ever. I knew if I married him, I had to stay. And I would. I had to face that consequence whatever it would manifest as. It always shows up as something.

The gut tug was all I had to go on at 21 years old. It was spot on in the eleventh hour. But it was spot on.

If I stayed, I would have developed a nasty disease or horrific illness early on. I saw it growing when I had a decision to make. If I had chosen marriage, I would have died early. I would have to come back and start this ride over. I am here for a reason.

Today, this amazing soul is one of my best friends. He was the angel who got me on the plane to join him for his reunion. That was the flight when I met Craig. I prayed for a knight in shining armor. John called. He told me to get on the plane. He wouldn't let up until I agreed. He was an angel pushing me hard to take that next step that I begged him to push me to take. I had to take that flight. I had no choice.

After an angel on the plane disappeared and a powerful gut tug in the form of a bomb, I met the man who would be the next breadcrumb on my path.

This is why I push you so hard. There is something amazing waiting for you. A man I loved dearly and trusted with my life insisted that I do something crazy and I had to "do it right now." There was no time to fear or ponder. I didn't need to bring anything but toiletries. Everything would be provided. I just had to go. A ticket was waiting at the counter.

When you face these intersections, you know your life will never be the same. But you asked for them to show up. The Extreme Vallarta Adventure I just went on was just this. You didn't have time to think. You just had to jump or go. Someone was roped in right behind you.

I had someone in my life. They scared me. This would end this story for sure. I was terrified. I wanted out. I went to the airport.

Two and a half years later, Craig brought me to Ohio. I found the path to my big-girl panties. Finding them took five and a half more years.

John O. has often been how I get back on track. A quick nudge, reminder, lane change. Then I don't hear from him for a year. I love it.

Craig and I sat together before this incarnation and planned our intersection. He would become a bodybuilder; it would change his life. My life would be so lost, sad, and alone in Ohio that I would force myself out of my comfort zone. Books helped. The hardest thing I did was stewing in thoughts about how I would escape life in Ohio. The thoughts. The doing was easy after months of self-torture. We can amazingly talk ourselves out of everything we know we need to do.

My book is about showing that it is not hard to leave a difficult situation. It is our "thinking" about it that makes it hard. Leaving is easy when you "know" it is time. When you "know" at the soul level, you will realize the hard work is already done. You planned it. There are no errors.

It is the thoughts you will torture yourself with that manifests dis-ease.

I did everything by trial and error, and instinct. Leaving John O. immediately set my soul free. The human had to mourn a few tears of confusion. The soul was at peace. He had to move on as he thought he had a perfect plan with me in the picture. He had to course correct, recalibrate, and find his new beginning.

I am happy to report that he is living the life of his dreams. It is full of beautiful people and clothing, riches and abundance. He's traveled the world. He had his Cinderella wedding. He has two daughters, who will both have the same. He said the only thing he and his wife disagreed on was if their education was to be strictly Ivy League.

I would have died in that life. I would have wanted to die. Those are conversations I don't want to hear.

I've sent him pictures from hiking, my fire pit, or paddleboarding in the mountains. His response is always, "Well, aren't you Nature Girl?" He loves five-star luxury and everything at the top of the line. I love hiking, mountains, and a roaring fire under the stars. We joke often about how different we are. We are exactly where we are supposed to be. His life is what he wanted it to be.

I was not the right fit for his story. We got to figure it out right away and not drag it out. In my book, I question if life would have been different if we didn't have the weight on our shoulders of "we have to get married." Perhaps if we moved to Boston and played for a while. Better yet, what if we stayed in LA as we were both already in management in the company? We were both so young.

It is that thought of the "expected" next step you take in life. I don't know what would have happened to us. I believe we would have evolved apart as those parts of us wouldn't match up. But I got to see it early. We got to miss out on having that fun together, but also the heartbreak we would have had to deal with.

No matter what, I believe listening once you hear the feeling is all you need. It is your guidance telling you to get back on track. Those aren't always butterflies of excitement, sugar.

And my life, oh my. It is spectacular and immaculate. I listened to only me and my gut my entire life. I never questioned. And now here I am. It is a solo ride because everyone else is stuck in a story and loaded with beliefs. I am not. I know why we are here and it is magnificent.

I never did become a catholic. That poor priest. For two weeks he had to listen to my questions. He was so frustrated. With an attempted smile, he would silently scream in my face, "JUST BELIEVE!" I said, "I need to believe what you are saying, just because you are telling me to?"

Lowering his head and sighing as if he thought I finally got it, he said, "Yes."

Right there, I saw what the problem is with this world.

In the place where I grew up, many married their high school sweetheart. As far as I know, many of these couples are still together and are quite happy according to Facebook. I hear so many love stories of people who have been in love for 50, or 75 years. I understand this. I totally get it. I know many couples who live a very vanilla life. They didn't have a horrible childhood. They didn't have tragedy. Their life was okay. Their partner's life was okay. The town they live in is okay. The job opportunities are good. Everything is fine. These people grow old together. It happens. When your world doesn't get rocked, you aren't looking for answers.

On their deathbeds, they will have regrets. They dream of that thing they secretly always wanted to see that they never saw. That place they wanted to go. That thing they wanted to do. They compromised at a young age, but it was okay because they were "the cards handed to you." You believed this. You think your life was your destiny. The person you met at sixteen was to be by your side, basically until your next life. Yes, it can be good and "feel good" when you do this, but you never get to see the life you could have had if you said yes to "you" first, and always. If we all did this, the world would be bliss.

You will have opportunities again to change the outcome of your unfinished stories. You are not done learning your lessons. We come back time and time again until we step out of the lesson. We must change the outcome.

We are not locked in for life. We are not supposed to be. We are supposed to do those things we wanted to do; no regrets. Why would you want to be dying and have regrets? Those things you wish you would have done, do them now. They are going to take you to the place you want to go. They're going to give you that next step in your life. You planned greatness for yourself. Stop selling yourself short.

If you had a vanilla life and you cruised Water Street, then graduated to Fremont Street, I hope you left town. At least for a while.

When your life is tragic, you become scrappy. You do everything in your power to survive. I know very few kids like that, but they are going to be powerful adults. This book is for two of them. Jonathan and Liam.

When we have a horrible past, the pendulum tends to swing a lot further in the other direction. We do not settle for vanilla. We have something pulling at us our entire life leading us to our potential. We know we have a plan, we know we have to follow our arrow, so we do. We are a lot more driven than those with a vanilla childhood. I am grateful for my tragedies. They lit a fire in me that will never stop burning.

The stuff I write is supposed to slap you into remembering who you are. You are so far from your reality. You have no idea where you came from or what your plan was, but you came here with a roadmap. You planned on finding your breadcrumb trail.

As I broadcast from my Mount Shasta location, I look at the planet and realize you guys have absolutely no idea what love is. You can't. The last two relationships I had were for them to learn a lesson. These two men were not to be part of my future. One was my Twin Flame. I know many of you hope to find your twin. It will be fully explained in Season Three of *Only Beautiful Things Happen to Me.*

Looking back at his reality, and his expectation of me was what most of you equate as love. Anything that I did before meeting him mattered. Since I didn't share anything, because it doesn't matter, he researched me on Facebook. He scrolled everywhere. I'm sure he googled me up and down.

What about my life yesterday is important today? The woman I was five weeks ago is nowhere near the woman I am today. He was so desperate to find my weaknesses.

He wanted to know everything about my history. Who I dated. He looked for patterns on where I put a "like" or "love" response on Facebook. He was desperate to find something to have on me. He had to have someone who was also damaged goods. He couldn't trust himself that he was enough. He had to find a lie somewhere. He couldn't. With me, what you see is exactly what you get.

He needed to own me. I can't be owned. Neither can you. He wanted to be a daddy to me. He wanted to read me bedtime stories and tuck me in. He wanted to show me love by buying me things, looking me in the eye, and saying in an almost threatening tone, "I am doing this for you (or buying this) because I love you, Cari." Making sure I knew "love" was the price he was paying and he needed it in return. I was all in. But he couldn't trust himself. He would tell me how his horrible heartbreaks brought on PTSD. I wasn't there to break anyone's heart. I didn't need stuff.

After our six weeks together, he gathered up every item he "gave" me as they were contingent on me loving him at any cost. Love had an actual price with this human.

He was constantly looking backward in my life to see who I was five, or ten years ago. Who I am now is all that matters. If we are judged by who were at any point in our existence, we would all be damned. We have all done things to grow and learn. And boy, I think I've learned more than most of you have. That's why I'm writing the books I'm writing. I can't believe the number of experience-compartments behind me in my life.

In your relationships, you are two broken souls who cling together to fill holes for each other. You believe you need each other. You do not have faith enough in yourself to exist without another. Not for a second would you think you are strong enough to go through life alone. I've got news for you. After you experience complete aloneness for a long enough time, you fall in love with who you become. It's being around people that is a challenge now. You all want to fight to stay stuck, and cannot believe life can be as brilliant as I describe. Your brain can't even join me here. Let alone the "belief" that you have the same power.

Marriage was a man-made creation involving dowries, property, and money. As long as you are committed to somebody at the soul level, they are yours. When the commitment or your story is over, you go your separate ways. Just being a couple is enough. Creating marriage, divorce, separation, alimony, and splitting children in half; it is crazy. When the "love" as you call it is gone, just end it. Walk away. Remember that you *did* love each other. You can't help but feel what you feel. Remember the way it felt when you started and know you each get to feel that feeling again.

Do not drag your children through a mud-slinging war. It is all just stuff. Divide, conquer, go. Be done with it. We are not crows.

Plain old insecurity, jealousy, anger, fear of being alone, and all kinds of abandonment issues arise when we see the end of a story. We want to cling to that sinking ship because we know we have what it takes to plug the holes. We can save us. Why would you want to? Stick a fork in it. You have better things coming to you when you walk out of an old worn-out story.

People love us, then they stop loving us. We are not meant to be with someone forever. I say we do away with any form of commitment language whatsoever. As long as you are authentically being honest, being who you are, and speaking your truth, you cannot not attract people who are exactly like you. If you find somebody that you love, you merge together, you have a wonderful time and an ending. Each ending is a brand-new beginning.

Saying "yes" to someone is not a death sentence. You are saying yes to what you feel at this moment. If you grow vibrationally together, you can last an eternity. If one of you grows while the other isn't worthy (believes it), you will feel the division between you growing larger. You can see it like a pie chart. You felt equal. Now, one of you is blaming, expecting, and not happy with who they are. You are growing in yellow as the red is shrinking. You need to remain at the same level or it cannot work. Don't let their inadequacy be your problem. They need to figure out who they are just as much as you need to figure out who you are.

Be with them until it is over. It is not what you must do for the rest of your days on this planet. Say goodbye to each other. Remember you came together from love; leave with love. Then find your next breadcrumb.

CHAPTER 15
MAKING BABIES

Why do we have children? Mostly because of unprotected sex. But when it's intentional, why do we have them? What is the endgame? To have a family. What exactly does that mean?

A family is what you make it. If you want to have babies, you need to be able to be a mother. And it's nice to have a father. But there are many combinations and ways to raise children.

What is your why?

I was never going to have children. I was abused as a child and a victim into my 30s. I was not going to bring a child into my victim-world because I would only create another victim. I knew without being okay with myself, how can I create a human that is okay? It was pretty cut and dry.

When I met John and we got married. We agreed if it was meant to be, it would be. We would give it a try since we were older parents going in. Apparently, it took quickly.

I knew at that time and age I was very equipped to be an amazing mother. I was no longer a victim. Strong, sure of myself, and I've been where everybody has been. I have been abused. I have been broken. I have had bill collectors harassing me. I watched our car get repossessed. I was held out of a helicopter at three over Hoover Dam. I was fed my pet rabbit. I was tortured, physically and sexually abused, and had to watch my mother be thrown across the house.

Before sixth grade, I gave two police depositions as a witness or victim to my mother's bad choices.

I was no longer any of that. I walked through every sad story that ever was mine, and I no longer own one bit of any of it. I knew I would be a beautiful example for my daughter to teach strength, resilience, and following your true north. One thing I didn't realize until much later was that yes, she saw how bad-ass tough I was. But there wasn't any part of my old life that leaked through. She couldn't see that once I was suicidal. She couldn't believe that the woman before her ever "suffered depression." Her mom was a rock.

When people hear stories of what some of my stepdads did to me, it sends them into a rage. I remind them that it was my normal. It was what I was used to. Look at me now! I wouldn't be this if it weren't for that. I grew from a tragic experience. I bless the experience and move on. I plead for them to not get stuck in one of my old and long-forgotten stories. Why should they carry hate energy about my story when they have enough to carry?

Below is a blog post I did recently about the miracle of creating life.

"You Forgot Miracles Exist."

I see a vision. I am holding a piece of black paper and two drops of water are added to the paper. In a moment, the two drops of water move together to become one. At that point, they cannot be separated. Which parts belong to which drop? It is all one. It is the first miracle. It is the last miracle for most of you.

How can you wrap your brains around the fact that you once started as two tiny little drops? One drop was labeled an egg and the other was labeled a seed. Names don't matter. Pay attention to the miracle.

When the time is right and the right seed is near the egg, they become a drop that cannot be separated. It isn't that the other sperm racing to get to the egg are good sperm or bad sperm, they just weren't the sperm that was to attach to this egg. Period. It is simple. The one that did is the one that was supposed to attach; none other. There are no errors.

As humans, we embrace the "Miracle of Childbirth." Then it's end-of-story. I find this fascinating.

Now I realize every part of life, beginning with childbirth is miraculous. I find it amazing that you experience the first moment and acknowledge the magic for a second, and then you put the Genie back in the bottle like it never came out. Wild.

Look around you. Every plant was once a seed flying through the air. Every tree was once part of a majestic tree somewhere far, far away. Everything finds a way to get to where it is needed. It always does. The only thing that can stop the natural flow of what is needed – is your human brain. Your inability to believe that there is so much more than you could comprehend.

The idea is that when you allow yourself to be fluid, you will find more drops you are to blend with; those you planned to bump into. Bumping into them is everything. It must be an in-person connection.

You will never find the drops that will complete and expand your universe by living the limited life you have accepted as normal. The people to the left of you do it. The people to the right of you do it. If you do something out of the box, they will look at you through another lens. They will judge you and question your reality. Watch out; you don't want that to happen. You do nothing. You wait until one of your neighbors does something crazy before you ignite your life into something magical. Or you die.

What your limited self cannot comprehend is that you need to be out discovering your arrow. It will take you to a land of uncharted territory.

When I followed guidance and went to Sedona, I met Alden. I had to get to Sedona as he was only going to be there for two days. After this, he would head back to the northeast and begin his death process. He was a drop that had to connect with this drop. We had to meet in person. By meeting it opened up sides of me that I couldn't have known could exist. It opened up a paranormal reality that makes my life Disneyland and Magic Mountain every single day.

I met the woman in Seal Rock. She had to meet me to have that part of her opened up. I had to meet John when I was young. He became my soul brother from another mother at 21 years old. He has been a critical part of my movement on this rock. He was not supposed to be my happy ever after; that was how we were to meet. He has been a driving force in where I go, how I got there, and who I've met.

A woman came to me for her awakening in December. We realized that even though we met many years ago, we were not at the space where we could exchange the gifts we had for each other yet. When she came in December, it was two drops of water on a paper that blended and the connection that was predestined was established. We both grew immensely from that second – in perfect timing – connection.

We are born and it is a miracle. Every next step and path that unfolds is also a miracle. You stopped believing in miracles somewhere along the way. Why? I am just now beginning to understand them. I can't get enough of the idea and the promise of more. I live them daily.

You immersed yourself into a reality that is harsh, sad, and painful. You cling to a community of "like-thinkers" and you know you cannot step outside of that box. You've dug a hole, and you call it your reality.

I'm here to tell you it is just a stupid hole. At any point, you can climb out of it. You are never stuck. When you change your mind, you can walk out. The only thing keeping you stuck is you. Not one other human or person has power or authority over you. The only power they have is the reins you have given them. Take your power back. Own your life. Not one other human can possibly know of the passion stirring inside of you. Show them. Don't die with it inside of you.

Life is a miracle. This planet is a miracle. How you exist can change with one simple thought. You choose to stay stuck because it is the popular opinion. You have no idea how good life can be when you let go of the reality you were told you needed to live. Not one part of it is real.

Get out. Change your mind. Find you. Prepare to be blown away.

The bottom line is we are here to create pretty magical stories. To continue on, we need babies. They are going to keep coming. You have family stories ahead that have yet to unfold. Try to raise them to be who they are. Not who you think they should be. You will know what I mean by the end of this book.

CHAPTER 16
HAVING A LEG UP

My ex-husband said a whole lot of things to me that made no sense, but this comment encouraged this book. He honestly believes and lives by what he said. It was the world he was raised in.

From the bottom of his heart, he believes it is important for your child to have an inheritance. He sees it as a foothold; an easy start to life in a hard world. He believes they need something that separates them from the rest. A "leg-up." The child with the nest egg is the winner. In his mind, this is his reality.

He didn't come from a world where that can't exist. I have been in both worlds. I know which one feels better.

This book is not only going to challenge his philosophy, it is going to destroy it.

I will argue this to the moon and back. I was born with nothing, and I knew I would receive nothing. I did end up inheriting one thing. A disease. But that was it. When I came through the birth canal with the help of Castor oil, to survive I had to have a plan. There was no 'plan' for me. There was no college tuition. There was no family business. There was no farm. I had to figure my life out. I never looked at this as a tragedy. I just didn't come with instructions.

How are we supposed to survive without a safety net? My mother was clueless. She was a horrible role model. I came to have this mom and to live this exact life. We come here to find our path, to let it unfold, and to continue walking on it until we no longer walk this earth.

I say giving them something to start with ruins them from the start. You give them a much larger hill to climb than I had. I was tortured. You're giving them comfort and ease. You're giving them an easy way to survive. You show them their world, "If you do this, this will happen. These are your instructions. And here's what you want to attain in your life" They tell you everything you need to do according to them. They paint a blank canvas called you and tell you, this is your life.

Like all kids, being young was hard for my daughter. We all have to squish and twist ourselves over and over to fit into a tube of toothpaste. We try hard to become what we believe we should be. Everyone shows us what is important in life. We carefully watch, learn, and analyze. Do I do what they do even though it feels icky to me? We want so much to be who we feel we are on the inside, but we are told what we need to be.

It is an impossible situation. When you tell your child what they are, rather than allow them to unfold naturally, you erase their canvas. You sterilize the dish so no parts of who they came here to be show up. You feed the thing you need it to be so what it wants to be never surfaces.

We did a "final family ski trip" when my daughter was in her senior year of college. It was after we returned home from this trip when my mother-in-law slipped and said something the mother of the child was not aware of.

Through high school, I wanted her to get a job. Get the experience of going to work, clocking in and out, seeing weekly paychecks, meeting different personalities, all of the things we experience by mingling with new strangers. Her dad was never on board with this. I was not informed until the slip by G-ma that she was getting paid to go to school by G-ma. Her inheritance started her freshman year. No one mentioned this little nugget to the mother.

Once I lost my shit and recomposed, I put my hands on the shoulders of my 'at the time' husband and said, "Do not interfere with their move to LA. Let them figure it out. This is their story, let them find the way. They need to budget, figure out expenses, know what they need, etc. Please, do not interject."

As always, he looked at me with a glaze and bobbing head, half smile, and agreed. He would say anything to move beyond this moment. The look was always the same.

Adulting means figuring things out. It means knowing what you are capable of doing within your means. When you have someone sprinkling "I love you this way" juice all over your life, it is hard to say, "Leave me alone. I want to figure this out." Having a cushion or a knowing that you will not fail is a beautiful feeling to carry. But it isn't reality. Keeping your paddles next to you is a safety net. It says to the world, "I am not enough on my own. I don't trust myself. I don't have faith in me without you."

What I wanted for my child to experience that he took away from her was a lesson in learning how to function, how to stand up for what you want, and how to explain your point. If you know you are moving to another city, there are a million things to consider. There is planning, knowing what you need in advance. This is a time that tests any human being. This is a time that destroys many couples. Anything that he did takes life lessons away from our child. She never had the chance to sit with her partner to "plan their move."

He took the time off of work, helped pack them, drove down with them, and helped them find the place, and move in. All of this is wrong.

What they didn't get to do was everything. They didn't get to fight about what a couple argues about in the planning phase. They didn't get to employ their internal guidance. They didn't get to talk about what mattered to them to come to an agreement on where they needed to be. What did the place need to feel like?

His stepping in at all interfered with their intuition. They never had their chance to feel their way to their next step.

My prediction early on was that they would never survive as a couple. They are both incredible humans, but they were not meant to be together for the long haul. They came to each other and gave each other a gift. They wouldn't have survived the move. They would have broken up at the end of college and gone their separate ways.

Because my ex made it easy, they went with the natural flow for them. When someone is doing it for you, you are not going to learn from it. As they say in Harry Potter, "Do what is right or what is easy." Doing what "feels" right to your core is the only answer.

Your guidance tells you where you need to be and when. But when someone is doing for you all the time, you can't find that space within that is reaching for a solution. The solutions are right there at all times. With help always at your fingertips, you cannot find them. It is simple.

By him having a huge hand in relocating his child, doing all of the heavy lifting, financial assistance, or otherwise, he is following what he believes is his guidance. He is taking away from them learning how to figure out how to pull all of this off on their own. What he is following is his natural-born training. But he is deciding or affecting the decisions by being in the way. They can't figure this out together when he keeps inserting his assistance.

I know he loves his kid, and he shows it by "doing" for her. She needs to learn how to do things without his help.

We must follow our internal guidance. It is always telling us where we need to be. When you come here as I did, you find your way. You make sure you find your way. You turn over every leaf until you figure out why you were brought here. And you find it. There is a place to go. There is an ending after all of the stories we come here to experience.

I came here with tragedy, trauma, horrible childhood, blah, blah, blah. I got through it. And then I thrived. Because I can. I chose my way here. Rather than remaining a victim, I flipped my script. I decided nobody else was going to pull up my big girl panties for me. It's time I put them on. And oh, did I ever. Oh yes, I did. I'm driving this bus and nobody can even get near it.

If you are born with a silver spoon, a college plan, preschool paid, and expectations, you are screwed. You have a big hill to climb. I can guarantee you that Ivanka, and Donald Jr., may be looking really sharp on Celebrity Apprentice, but there are parts of them inside that just want to explode into who they wanted to be as a little kid. But even as a little kid, they were told what they had to be. That's what happened to The Donald.

Our story gets so convoluted because we have no idea who we are at the end of our programming. We have become programmed human beings. Raised and farmed into what is needed on this planet. You want to be part of the one percent. It looks really pretty from the ground.

You have a lobotomy before you're even born. You can never become who you came here to be. You will be what you are told.

CHAPTER 17
PROGRAMMING

I never considered myself to be proficient enough that I could write a book without lots of editing assistance. My confidence was very low. I subscribed to Grammarly and started using it for all of my translating-to-proper-English needs.

I am not exposed to what's happening on the planet. I do have social media, and with many of the different applications, I am invited to use AI. I don't even go there. I have plenty to say without it doing the work for me. It can't know what I want to write

Grammarly started to not make sense. I started to notice corrections were nothing like before. For the longest time, I surrendered to Grammarly. I completely depended on it. Then I started to second-guess it to the point where I unsubscribed.

I no longer use it. I now trust what I know more than what is outside of me. Like the "corrections" on my iPhone, offering a misspelled word or to use the same word twice. I now trust that what comes through me is the best possible version of what I have to say. I know doing the dictation that I do now, there are so many commas inserted between everything I write. I know I can't keep on top of all of it. These are your robots running our planet.

I want to take this a step further. I was born poor, and free. There was nothing telling me what I could, or could not be. I had to decide to own my life.

Once you smash through potty training, you are already slated to begin your career at the 'right' preschool. You were enrolled before you were born. Then, you enter into the school district with the most opportunities for your favorite child. The right college, the right direction, the right family, the right expectations You are doing exactly what they are programming you to do. You are being spoon-fed your future. It doesn't feel okay and you can't put your finger on why. I can.

You came here with a plan. You are a living, breathing being. You had an instinctual direction you were headed. You were groomed into a role that they needed and expected you to fill. How is this okay with you? You have become their robot. They have trained you on how to be a little mini-me to represent them – and the life *they feel is important*. How much of their reality makes you feel all ooey gooey inside with happy tingles? I know getting that new ____ feels good for a second, but overall, there is something in you aching to be set free.

To them, clearly, your life isn't important. Do you see that perhaps you are a utility for someone? You fill a function. What does a close family feel like to you? How do you show love for one another? Is there respect across the board? Do you fear anyone in your family?

There are many questions you need to ask yourself. If you don't go the direction the family trained you to go, what happens? I'm dying to know.

I wouldn't take too deep of a personal inventory because you already know when you're in a world that does not feel right. You go through the motions because it is what you have to do. I'm telling you, you don't.

Seeing a limousine on the freeway in Seattle long, long ago brought to mind, "Just for one day it would be fun to live like a filthy rich person." To shop and to know you are not limited. If you want it, you can buy it. To not factor in traffic or the best route. You have a driver. You pretend to become best friends with them although they are nothing like you. They don't want to be like you. You think they envy you. That was many years ago. With what I have and my precious life, I would never want to test-drive your shoes now.

You can't judge a man unless you walk a country mile in his shoes; a line from a Zac Brown song. You can't judge a man ever. But looking at the limousine fantasy long ago, I really thought I would want to see what it felt like. To be so unlimited that you can go anywhere, do anything, and not have to think about anything.

As I have grown into a spiritual being who wants for nothing, the more I realize I would never want to spend a minute in your shoes. I can't even be around those of you who believe you are significant humans. Just because you were raised that way and taught that you shine brighter than another, I can't agree with you. I cannot be around you. It's just icky energy as far as I am concerned. You are lying to yourself, and so there's no way in hell I can have a conversation with you.

You are nowhere near who you are. No one knows this more than you do. But you have absolutely no idea how to get to where you want to be. You put on the costume, you wear the make-up, and you play the part. But the part feels off. You don't want to do this. This is not who you want to be. But you have to be this. You believe you have no choice.

In every book, I talk about beliefs. How when you change your thoughts, you change your life. A belief is a thought you continue to think. If you think you have to stay put somewhere for whatever reason, you do. Leaving would be the devastation you imagine it would be. Or, you could change your mind. You can reach that side of you filled with passion and let it drive your soul. That side of you is your roadmap. That side of you is waiting for you to acknowledge its existence. That side of you is screaming at you to take control of your life. But, you're too afraid. There is too much power over you. You have too much to lose. Everything is real as long as you believe it. I've got great news for you.

What you're about to read is going to give you a ticket out of anything you no longer wish to be part of. You get to start saying no to everything you had to say yes to. You get to expect people to honor your decisions. If they don't honor you following your path, you do not want them standing before you, do you? Wouldn't that be the dumbest thing you've ever done? Having somebody disrespect what you believe in and what you want to do. You would never do that to anybody, would you? Have you? Why?

Whatever you were born into, whatever you were told you had to be, it's all a lie. You don't have to be anything. As a matter of fact, you are going down the wrong path. The further down the road you go, the more you are unbecoming you. The sooner you turn your thoughts around, the sooner you can find your way out of the tunnel.

Oh, the thoughts that will spin through your head if you slip into the thoughts, "Can I really leave?" You will visualize every possible disaster scenario imaginable. There will be tunnels filled with darkness and doors to nowhere. You will never find your way out. It will be too daunting. It will not be worth your time. You would rather die than put effort into a chance of living your way. Rather, you die a slow, miserable death being someone you can't recognize.

And the bad news is You do know this is all a play, correct? You know you come back here time, and time again, learning lessons. And then you go home. You check in and you see what you learned, then you come back to do another lesson or rinse/repeat for the umpteenth time. You repeat lessons until you get through them.

You could be stuck in one story because you didn't say yes to you for centuries! When you get to the point where you say yes to you, that is when you move out of a story. You get your graduate degree and you move into the next story. You will learn this in all of my writing and videos.

Anything that makes you feel miserable in your gut is the thing you need to change. The more you deny its presence, the more you are causing a life of denial, disease, and discomfort. Or you will just drop dead. Maybe you are manifesting a horrible car accident.

You start believing that "ending it all" is the best way to go. That's what many of you do. You are in a life you don't want to be in and you ***believe you have no control***. As I said, your beliefs are everything. You always have control. If it doesn't feel right for you, it is not your journey.

You are here to represent one entity; the consciousness you call you.

You cannot know what others need to do, and they cannot know what you need to do. Just because you were born into it does not mean you own it. You own it if you claim it. When you declare, "That's not mine!" It is no longer yours. Then you feel a field of butterflies filling up your soul with giddiness and excitement. When you slip into your lane, it immediately feels perfect. You know you are in alignment with your plan. The plan you came here to find. For the age-old question that you want the answer to, yet you really don't want the answer. This is why we are here.

The simple reality is you are born into varied realities. If you were born into a reality where they planned preschool before you were born, going to college is the obvious next step, and often school beyond. Most of your young years have been laid out and predetermined. You didn't have a say in your life. Good luck.

How are we different from AI? Some of you may have heartfelt emotion, but you have been hard-wired and programmed all of your life. You are basically a computer. You've had download after download, you've sucked it all in, you've assumed it as yours. You've said yes to all of it. I'm telling you it is wrong.

We come with our software already installed. We have programming. It is the program we came here to decode. It's what we know. We come here to do this each lifetime. We pre-plan it. We have a goal. We know where we want to get to when we are born. We always know at the soul level.

This is why we feel icky when we aren't going in our direction. We also know we planned for obstacles to come at us. We created these situations. They are getting in front of our path intending to help us not get where we want to go. Or, poking and prodding at us to leave somewhere that we've overstayed our need to be there. We don't make it easy. I'm telling you following the things that feel good is all you should be doing. If you are being poked, pay attention! It is a sign. If someone keeps coming at you and it seems like it will never stop, you asked them to. They are helping you move on. Don't be stuck.

For many of you, it's being born somewhere where you have a leg up. That leg-up is not your friend. It is one doozewhoppy of an obstacle. It is one of the hardest situations to step away from to find your inner peace. But it is the only way you can find that sanctuary within. The only way to God is from the interior castle. You know you must access that dark part of you that you wish to keep in a box.

We have to live our lives by following our internal guidance system. When somebody else's guidance predetermines what your next steps are, how are you going to find the way home? It is going to be hard. That is why this book has to come out.

The only way to untangle a mess that has been made of your life before you even came here is for you to take charge of it right now. Throw down the designer handbag and lose the need for designer shoes. Get a pair of hikers. Step into nature and bury your feet in the sand. Walk in the water. Put on a tank top and flip-flops and go out to nature. Don't have anyone around you. Especially your bodyguards. Anyone to remind you that you're not who you want to be. Keep everyone away from you who wants to remind you that your duty is in their hands. This is incorrect.

So, simply put, if every single one of us was left alone at birth, taken care of, and kept alive This world would be full of happy people. Everybody would naturally follow their arrow and find their path. They would know who they are because they know who they are. They would not have someone telling them that they are not worthy to be who they think they are.

We are programmed by what people think of us. We are programmed by the plans they have for us. We cannot have any of our own ideas or thoughts. Our parents did the best they could based on what they had from their two sets of relatives.

We came from two sets of parents, who also came from two sets of parents, who also came from two sets of parents, and so on. We bring all of our garbage and their garbage forward with us. I'm saying let go of the garbage. All your parents had to do was get you removed from your mother's womb. The rest you can handle. But first, you have to be an infant, so they want to coddle you and tell you how limited you are.

They have no idea.

And then they tell you your future. They tell you what you might want to be when you grow up. They start showing you all the different career options and the different codes attached to them so you can follow your intended career path.

We know at a very young age what our strengths are and what we see ourselves doing. But when we act it out or pretend it is real, \ we are told that it is silly, shameful, stupid, fill in the blank. The file folder is created early on about "what we cannot be or do." We are told all kinds of ridiculous things. They become our reality. Where else can it come from?

The bottom line; we are naturally who we are when we are young. The older we get, the more crap we've heard from other people. We put importance on things that we didn't realize were important when we had our own mind. When we no longer use our mind, we find things special that were never special to us. You start learning from your leaders what you must achieve or buy in order to find the happy space they declare is the direction. Even then you know it isn't right. But you learn to trust to do what you are told.

You are a programmed, living, breathing being. We have heard there are robots and aliens among the living, but you are an actual programmed human being. You have an installed operating system that is not who you are. It has all kinds of bugs. It is not a happy software. It is not the one you intended to operate through in this lifetime.

You allowed them to install it. Every day you continue to allow them to further install all the messages and programming to let you know who you are. And you need to remember, it's not about you. You are part of their collective agreement. You were born because they needed you.

But you do have the power in your Ruby slippers to say, "Oh hell no. I am an individual. I am a solo operating system. I am not here to work for you. I am to find out what I am here to do. I am to find out who I'm here to help. I am not your robot. I will not do what you tell me to do. I was born alone and naked, and I'm heading out that way. I do not need you."

The moment we are born our plan is already set in motion. Our world becomes magical when we follow our plan. As soon as we can feed and dress ourselves, mother bird needs to kick us out of the nest. We already know where we need to go.

She might not have the chance. We may decide to circumnavigate the globe alone in a sailboat at sixteen years old. We may play piano like a master or swing a golf club like we've done for decades, at two years old. When we are allowed to become who we are, we become it. When we know, we know.

The only way we can find the path to where we are going is by disconnecting from everyone and everything that takes up real estate in your brain. Take the time to decompress, unplug, and revisit that little kid in you who had lots of dreams.

Remember, the ones telling you who you are need to do the same thing you are doing. They are operating out of habit. They also have a silent space and a silent life that would be ridden with shame if it were to be exposed. In a world of power and money, you will never know who is behind any of the masks.

When we are plugged into anything outside of ourselves, we can't access our reality. We can't. We are plugged into all the needs of all the others that we 'believe" is our job to take care of. We can never fully plug in to advance ourselves. It's impossible. We have so many self-assigned duties we think we must fulfill. We don't have any. The only one you are here to find and to untangle is the one in your skin bag. Who are you? Do you even have a clue? You are about to find out.

When the mother pushes you out of the nest, it's scary. That's exactly what you want it to feel like. That fear will take you to your answer.

CHAPTER 18
THE DENTIST

This is a small example of how my life works. There are no errors. I am always completely open and in surrender. When I'm told where to go, off I go. When I'm told it's not time, I don't go.

I was due to go to the dentist in Puyallup on April 2. We had to constantly reschedule because of my weather issues getting there. The highest pass on all of I-5 is between me and Medford. After rescheduling four times, I was finally set for April 2. The weather would be fine.

On March 11, I started getting a horrible toothache. I don't get toothaches. It felt like it could be the Implant the dentist installed last year. I reached out to see if I could get in sooner. I listen when my body speaks. I don't go to doctors; I don't have problems there. I can't. I can't be ill.

They were able to get me in on Friday at two. I knew this was the new plan.

The next morning, no toothache. As a matter of fact, it never hurt again. But I was going. The plan was in motion. A fun trip, uncovered because of it. It always does.

When I was there, they took X-rays, poked, prodded, and cleaned it, and there was nothing wrong with my tooth.

It was fascinating. I even identified which fang it was. I knew where the problem was. There was no pain the next day.

As I was taking my sweet time to do a coastal trip to get back home to Mount Shasta, something hit me. I had a good laugh. There are no mistakes in my life. Things happen for a reason.

I had an appointment on April 2. I did not have a problem or a toothache. I knew immediately that I had to get to the dentist early. I had to free myself up because, on April 2, my life was going to be busy elsewhere. I would be headed down another mystery path. I had to clean my slate and free myself up. And now after this morning's download, everything is happening. I cannot begin to tell you what is next for me. I'm always the last to know and the first to go.

I had to free my schedule as an entire book was going to come through me. I would become a dictating machine.

CHAPTER 19
SAY 'YES' TO YOU

We're always looking up to something else for permission, guidance, and a helping hand. What do we do now? We're all flailing in a universe of people who are all skin bags floating around not being sure what to do. Let's look at what has worked in the past.

Native Americans came here, and they learned from the land. They speak with the land. They are one with the earth. They know how to take care of our country. They listened, learned, and pretty much wrote the book on how to take care of all of us and sustain the planet. And then white man came in and did not listen. We destroyed it.

Many people look up to the heavens, looking to God for guidance, strength, and a finger to show the way. God was the way. In our country, we elected a leader. They would become the local, touchable, real human that we could look up to and call our leader. We knew they would never lead us astray. We would be safe with this leader.

We are a country and a planet full of flailing people who do not know where to look any longer. We looked to God, and then church destroyed our taste for God. Hearing different translations can be very confusing. The president is not someone we can look at to protect us and keep us safe. The only one we have is in our interior castle. Most of us don't know how to access this place. We've never known. That is why I am writing the books that I am writing. You have to find your interior space. You've given everything of yours away to the outside world. And you have no idea who you are.

We looked up to God. We looked up to the president. Now for some reason, we look up to the ivory towers. We look to power and money for permission. We look to power and money for our next step. We are now praying to a machine that is destroying our planet. I knew someone who wanted to be a filmmaker when the writers' strike was underway. I suggested they get the camera and go shake things up a bit with this suggestion, meanwhile rolling film.

When the writers held up their signs during the strike, they were holding these signs up to glass castles and ivory towers. They were not holding them up to a person. They held them up as if saying to OZ, "If you please sir, can you please allow us to do what we are gifted to do and not replace us with robots? We will patiently do nothing and await your answer." My immediate gut instinct was to turn to each other. Talk about how you can take what you have as a unit and start all over again without a "Management Level" that is unnecessary. You are the talent here. You can rebuild. Only reinvent the wheel when the time is right. Know when the time is right. This is the time.

Rather, you hold your signs and pray to the towers that the board convenes when they return from holiday. They hope they will think about the little guy on the street for a second. You know, the guy who actually "does the work." You. You pray to this mystery thing up in the sky which is power and money. This is the planet we have created.

It was so much simpler when we all believed in God. I wasn't even one of you. I was an abused kid, but it was easier knowing where the pain came from.

Now no one knows what to believe. They're researching everything under the sun because they have a screen in their hand. They know everything because they have information at their fingertips. Why did this become important? Can't you just surrender, trust, and believe that you will know your own way?

We have gone mad. We are praising rich people and putting them on pedestals. The rich are getting richer. Making you poor. You're poorer now than you've ever been. The disparity between them and us is ridiculous. But you keep saying it's okay. You keep saying it is okay to make the rich and powerful, richer and more powerful, which gives all of your power away.

"C'mon people, now smile on your brother everybody get together try to love one another right now."

You are so in the middle of this story that you can't see you are in the middle of a bad story. This is why I have been pulled aside to be silent so I can see things that you can't see. I was one of you. I lived in a big house. I had a creek in my backyard and a bridge. I drove nice cars. I lived in a world that I did not grow up in. And it felt so different. It felt so wrong. We were so comfortable that we could have anything that we wanted. We didn't have to fix things because we could easily afford to hire professionals.

In my old life that wasn't even a dream. I've lived both lives during this lifetime. Being scrappy and poor made me strong and resilient. Having a leg up gives you just that. You have a leg up. But your soul is missing so much of you. Your strength, your resiliency, your power, your individuality, and your independence. You have so much power and strength within you, but it had to be put to rest so you could be the person they needed to create. You have been made into something that you are not. You have no idea who you are. You have not met you yet. You will by the time you finish this book.

The last time you were even close to knowing yourself was when you were a child. When you dreamed of what you would be on this planet. You were a superhero. You had things you wanted to do. You and your invisible friend were going to conquer the world. But then you were told what you had to do and the dream had to go away. You were told your friend wasn't real. You were so confused because it was so real to you. It was real.

As a child, you are closer to spirit. It goes away as we assume more of the human reality. Everything you remember as magical from your early years was there for a reason. It was magical. It can still be magical. You need to go back to those files and once again open them up. Look through them. See what you are missing. Remember what you forgot.

I have to be quiet to write these books to tell you why we are here. When we are alone with us, we find the most beautiful magic within us. It's inside of us. But it is buried. You are so deep in your story that you can't see it. You can't even feel the reality of it. It can't be real. You are what **they have created** and this is your role. You do not know how to step out of this position.

I'm giving you permission to look within. Start there. You are the person you were meant to be. When you were a little child, you wanted to be something special. And it was something really simple. You were so good at it. You knew it was who you are; who you were to grow up to be, and how you would help this planet. Go back there. Go to those feelings. Remember what you came here to be. It was not pretend. It was not a dream or a game. It was the future. Go there.

Talk to that young child of yours. Who are you? What is missing in your life? Unless you lived in a world like Don Jr. or Ivanka, you did not dream of being rich and powerful. With the blink of an eye, you can have the reality you are missing. It doesn't have to take months to plan and strategize your exit interview. The world you dreamed of is right before you; you must say yes to it.

The thought of leaving any situation is hard, or almost impossible. It is when you feel to your core that you are on the wrong path that you must take action. If you don't, you will manifest all kinds of nasty dis-ease into your life.

When you know at the soul level that it is time to do something, the work is done for you. It truly is. Go to your soul, love yourself, have faith, believe in yourself, and say 'yes' to you. Say 'yes' to that thing that has always been you. Saying yes does the work for you.

Change is scary. It's the scariest thing on the planet. That's why people don't do it. It is the only thing that can take you to your Holy Grail. You have to push beyond your comfort zone.

Change became easy for me because the alternative certainly wasn't working. Accepting change, trusting that I did not set myself up for a shitty ride; I did not disappoint. I have so much beauty and magic in my life because I shut up and I only listen to me.

We have to be alone to find ourselves. You can't find "you" with the device in your hand, watching the news, or talking to everybody about everything that's going on. That just keeps the old icky stuff active. Everything you talk about you are keeping alive. Walk away from everything that does not serve you and you'll stop feeding the monster. Take your fork out of its mouth. Step away.

CHAPTER 20
WRITER'S STRIKE

There are times when the only option is to throw out the old way things were done and start anew. We need to reinvent the wheel. We need to change the way we do things. It is not working.

During the writer's strike, I knew someone who already wasn't working. I heard all about the reasons for the strike. Everyone that I asked during that time, "Who is on the other side of the strike? Who are they holding the signs up to?" This has always been clear in our world. Man versus company, union versus company, I did not get an answer from anybody. Nobody really knew who they were fighting.

What came through me as clear as a bell was this. The talent, the people who actually write the words that change our lives are holding up signs to "the man," whoever he is. Without talented writers, there are no storylines. They are the bread and butter of the writer's industry.

I suggested to this person that they go to the picket line with this suggestion. Tell everyone to put their signs down. Stop looking up to the window in the high-rise. Lower your sign. Lower your gaze and turn toward each other; once again be the gifted writers that they are. Pull a Taylor Swift. Re-create how you work. Improve your system. Get rid of the layers that don't serve you. Take back your power. Do not give your power away to an engine room full of rich people deciding your fate. Know without you it will not survive.

Why should they have to fight for the right to do what they naturally do? They need to gather together and walk away from the engine that has been supporting them. They need to stop the madness. Gather amongst themselves.

I am saying the same thing to you. We are all on the ground level. Our tower is not going to topple. We can't fall from the bottom. We can step away from anything anytime we want. Don't you think it's time? Take back our power. Why do we look at these glass towers and praise them and treat the people like they are royalty? They are self-appointed. But we agreed to their significance. You need to look in the mirror. We have this new breed of humans because you like having them to look at.

I am so grateful that I grew up in the little town of Henderson and Las Vegas, Nevada when I did. It was a pretty magical time back then. Yes, there was the mafia. There's always been something. But it was a place for families. It was where entertainers came to express and be born. It was magical. It felt as if everybody was equal. It had a small-town feel to it and it felt good.

Leaving was easy as it was so hot, but it was so cheap and easy to get back there to visit. It was always something to look forward to. I would see my sister, my old friend, we'd go to the lake and get Mexican food at Macayo's. It was the ritual. Buffets were cheap. Parking was free. Flights were cheap. It was never a big undertaking to fly home to Las Vegas. Now, it has become overpriced. The energy has shifted. I don't know if I will ever return.

When the "clubbing scene" took over, people would pay whatever it took to be in the same club as Lindsey Lohan or

Kim Kardashian. These celebrities you created were paid around $150,000 to simply be at the club. You made this important. This was no longer Vegas where I was raised.

People would stand in line to be in a club with these celebrities. Of course, the paparazzi were everywhere they were. This became your priority. You wanted to be where these people were. Somehow, they became something very important to you. You gave them incredible power.

They were the powerful people. They were significant. And you created this. Can you not see how you have created this craziness that made people like the Kardashian and Hilton royalty? They are no different than you or me. But you made them different.

You created a level of class that didn't exist before your beliefs pumped them up. And now I will never see front-row tickets again. I would not want to be in the Golden Circle with these people. I don't like these people; the energy would be like polarized batteries. Anyone who thinks they are better than anyone, their energy is very icky to me. It reminds me of Pigpen on Charlie Brown. They're like a big dirt ball in my space. Their energy is dark and ugly. I cannot be around it.

CHAPTER 21
REMEMBER EQUAL FOOTING?

What young people today will never comprehend; I remember fondly. It's as if it was just yesterday. Wait. I believe it was. How long ago did Blake Shelton and Miranda Lambert split up? When was the last time Adele came to Seattle before 2018? It wasn't that long ago. It was all before my daughter graduated from high school.

But what you have created is changing the playing field. The good old days were in the last decade; in the last ten years! They were the "Golden Days" when we were all on equal footing. We were all one. We all had a fair chance at everything. These days no longer exist. You will never know them.

Power and money did not rule the world. I had amazing luck and juju when it came to getting concert tickets. I got front row seats many times where I paid the same amount as the guy in the back row on the floor. Now those of us who can't afford the ridiculous front-row prices are stuck in the nosebleed sections. Why? Because you decided the rich and powerful should have the front rows reserved for them. They are special.

It seems like overnight; everything now is real estate for the rich and powerful only, pushing you and me down to the bottom of the Titanic. You could get the front row. You could get a good seat at a table at a restaurant. Everything was balanced. Everything was equal. You didn't have to be special or grease palms unless you were in Las Vegas. And now money equals front, and better. The rest of us will never go to the front again. And you are okay with this.

I bought four tickets to Blake Shelton and got center of the 12th row. When I saw the seating chart and realized I had the four tickets at the end of the catwalk, I did what I was going to do anyway. I put two of the seats on eBay. I paid $56 per ticket. Some man who wanted to impress a young woman spent $750 on eBay to get my other tickets. It became a bidding war. I don't have a problem with this. I would never pay for it.

We got fence-hugging front row for Miranda Lambert, front row for LeAnn Rimes, Carrie Underwood, and Trace Adkins. I worked in radio and yes, frequently we got tickets. They were not good tickets. They were off to the side. Winners got the good stuff. This is why I started getting them myself on Ticketmaster. It was a breeze.

These golden days had one price for floor seats, and one price for side seats. The nose-bleed section had a price, as well as box seats and suites. Everything had a price. You knew what everything cost upfront. It was the time when you could treat yourself and fly first class or stick to coach. You had two choices.

A few years ago, I was able to "own" things like Scrivener and Microsoft Word. I have a laptop that I will not part with because I am not going to pay a monthly fee for something I have always owned. I bought Scrivener on my old laptop when I first wrote my book in 2017. When I went back to log in on my new laptop, I no longer owned it. I must pay a subscription fee to go back to the thing I already bought and paid for.

Don't even get me started on the music I loaded on my computer from my CDs. Then iTunes went bye-bye. I no longer owned my music. Network TV and cable were the thing. You could buy movies or other specialty channels. Streaming services started. Movies were made for the theater or special TV nights. Now, you don't know what to watch or where to go. It is all over the place.

I have a singer/songwriter friend who was using her Spotify income to help with bills. She is the talent behind music. The one who lives the life in order to create powerful pieces. You know, a writer? Then, the day came when she was notified that she would no longer receive the royalties for her music. Excuse me. What? Who is getting paid for her songs? Why aren't we all thinking this way? Someone is getting paid for the work she did. We are allowing this.

I've created many videos on a few YouTube channels, and someone somewhere is making money off of them. It certainly isn't me.

I was pretty anal when I was young because I learned how to balance a checkbook. I would balance it monthly after the statement came in the mail. I would stay until I found the final penny. If I was off, I would not rest.

I realize that my child can't have any idea how to manage money. I had bill collectors calling me when I was a young girl because I did not have a role model. I was a financial disaster. It was easy to only pay $10 a month.

Today with subscription fees, streaming, and service fees, how can they keep track? I don't think anyone has a clue how much they are paying per month. My mother-in-law used to send checks to every charity that sent her a letter. She didn't realize she was on a monthly or annual recurring payment until her son looked at her checkbook.

I hate what we have become. Nickle and diming us to death so other people can have a monthly check delivered to the penthouse. We agree to it. We are keeping this bullshit alive. I want to pay what it costs right now. Tell me how much it costs, and our transaction is complete. Let's be done. I am not going to pay tuition or your car payment so I can have a _____. We have got to stop this.

Yes, we had a pandemic. Look at us. We needed a wake-up call. Why? Because you said it is okay to give more energy to the rich and powerful.

Because you decided that the rich and powerful should be idolized and put on a pedestal. You have created the "golden circle." You gave our seats away. People like me who got front row or close to front row seats every time will never have this chance again. We have turned this into a class system based on who has the most and is willing to spend it. Ticket levels are based on price, based on status. Those of us who still want a good deal better enjoy the Jumbotron. I will never attend a show again, I'm sure scalpers are still making a lovely living.

When was the last time you flew somewhere? I am grateful that I can fit into a suitcase. I have no problem being crammed into a window seat. I prefer the window. Depending on how much you are willing to pay – or what "add-ons" you might require during your flight, you will be in the back of the plane. You will always scurry by those in the other classes who were able to board before you. I remember when we did the logical thing, not the thing money can buy. We loaded the back of the plane first. Now, it depends on money and class.

I know many people earn miles for business; this is generally speaking. We have turned away from those "with" and those "without." Now we are a fuzzy line with a whole lot of us doing and going without. But you are creating it. You are praising power.

Life was equal and we all had the same chance. People like me or you could accidentally get a ticket upfront. It happened all the time. What are the chances of you ever seeing the front row again? Do you know someone? Are you connected?

This world has gone to hell in a handbasket. We have decided that the days when everybody gets a fair shot are gone. A fair shot is out the window. Who you are, how much money and power you have, and who you are connected to determines what you get. And the little guy has agreed to it. The little guy praising your world is who gives you your power. You are loving every minute of it.

I can't watch TV but what you people like to watch and spend your time on is what has created the problem. Can you not see the damage you are doing? Why do the lives of housewives or rich kids matter to anyone? These are not housewives. You are saying the people who have money are the smart ones. They are the ones to be like. They are the ones to follow. They must know much more than you because they are so connected. You have given your life away so they can have the front row. I do not agree with you.

We are all the same. Just like the purple people in the story. It's how we adorn ourselves that makes us different. It's what we believe about who we are that separates us. If we believe we are better than someone else, then it takes us to a mental space where we believe it. We have been told how special we are by so many people, clearly, it must be a fact. When in fact, we all came here naked. We all came here and burst into tears, and filled many diapers. We all came here on the same playing field. The difference is what we as a collective have decided is okay and what is not.

I had the concert ticket juju when my daughter was young. Her friend Laurel got to attend her very first concert, and it just happened to be in the front row. This will never happen again because of how you guys decided it must be. You want to praise and worship those who are on stage or have power and money, because you decided that is what is important. Just because someone can carry a tune and put on an amazing stage experience (thanks to money), you praise them. The actor who reads a line, you praise them. We can all sing and act. No one is special.

It puts you down on the bottom of the ship, but you are okay with being on the bottom. As long as you can keep watching your programs and television shows, you are complete. You shall live your life vicariously through them. You must continue to celebrate them as humans. Clearly, they know the right way because they have _____. What do they have? What makes them special? Why are you letting them push you down into a lower-class system?

I guarantee what you think you want is not what you want. You have been programmed since before you were born. When mommy and daddy were talking to you while you were still in the tummy, you were hearing what your life would look like. The baby heard and was programmed early on. It didn't matter what it came here with; the skill set that baby knew it needed to bring to the surface. You unplugged it before it was born. You decided your needs were more important than what they brought to the planet. You never let it unveil who it is. You kept telling it what it was.

This child could never have wants and needs. It is not an independent human being. It is part of your team. We have grown into a world of teams and collaboration, and the individual is gone. The human element is no longer necessary. What each individual brings to the party no longer matters. We are programmed machines. We are in our own universe. You truly have no idea who you are.

I speak these words with full authority because I've been you. I was the poor kid who watched her car be dragged down the street when we couldn't make the payments. I lived in low-income housing, multiple times, with my sisters stacked on top of me. I've lived an abundant life with wealth and the ability to do anything or go anywhere. I've been everywhere in between.

I am back to the basics of life, appreciating my natural and outdoor space. I spend my time where it feels magical here at the root chakra of the planet. What is important and our values are crystal clear here. We come here to operate from a space of love. We are born with birds and bees, and dogs and cats. We are born to immerse ourselves in nature. We are part of nature. We are not here to destroy it.

As I sit in the country, I'm back to what is important. When you let go of what you were taught you were, you find your way home. You find that missing part. You appreciate the smallest flower or the passing butterfly. You see the flowers on the tree and know the apples are going to be abundant. You play games with ground squirrels to see who is going to win the war. Meanwhile harming nothing.

When you come from a place of love, love comes back to you. And you become abundant. Your soul fills you with everything that you've been missing you thought came from outside. Love comes from within. When you get back to you, your cup runneth over with appreciation, gratitude, and self-love. You will never look back to what you thought mattered again. You will find the only thing that matters is when your soul is full. When you feed your soul, you know that is the only thing that you've ever needed to do. Once you do that, everything you need to take you to your path will appear before you.

You need to come from a place of love. Not a false God. Not false prophets. Not castles you created and declared as important. They do not matter. Nothing matters. They've been waving their hands in the air saying look at me. And you do. You can't take your eyes off of them. Now you want to be like them. How did this happen? What happened to the parts of you that are special? What happened to what you loved about you?

For most of us, it was lost early in our childhood. Those moments that made us giggle because we were excited about being grown-up were shattered by the world we were inheriting. There would be no room for us to be us.

Let's get one thing perfectly clear. No matter what story you are in the middle of, you are not a victim. You are never stuck. Stuck is a choice; a lazy decision. I don't care what the story is. He's in jail, you done her wrong, that ain't my baby, my husband dresses me, my mommy made me do it, you need a paternity test whatever crazy story you are in, you chose your way where you are. No one brought you to the story you walk in except for you. You had to say yes to get there.

When we start owning this reality, we can start doing something about it. When we think pointing our finger at you is the answer, deflecting the truth from us, it merely delays our growth. Pointing the finger throws energy outside of your responsibility realm. But you are the only one responsible for you. You are creating an ick-fest of nasty energy. Own your life. Stop pointing elsewhere.

No matter what your situation is, you choose it. If it is really bad and there's nowhere for you to go, you choose it. There's always somewhere to go. You do not have to defer to other people to find your way out of anything. Find your way through the inside. Listen to the only one who can possibly know their way through your world.

The only one who could possibly know is the one behind the eyes, ears, mouth, heart, and lungs. The one behind the fingertips. Who is feeling what you touch? Who is seeing what you see? There is so much more to you than meets the eye. What is inside of the skin is just a portion of your sparkle. The rest of you surrounds your body. That magnificent portion of you is your puppet master. They are trying to point you in the right direction. So am I. We hope you sense the way we are pointing.

When you see the way and you take one step, you will feel in alignment for the first time in your life. Once you follow that one footstep, that one breadcrumb, you can't wait to know what is next. Then, the next step will show up. You are not alone. You are never alone. There are no errors. This is the path you planned on taking. The breadcrumbs are all lined up for you. You just needed to say yes.

On cruises, everybody ate in the same massive dining room and had the same choices of food, and it was included in the price. Now you have expensive steak houses, French restaurants, and things that the rich can afford outside of our budget. Meanwhile, the really rich and really powerful have their own restaurants because we don't want them anywhere near us. They think it's the other way around.

I think I liked it when we were all blended together in the same bag of rich, poor, and in-between. We felt much more equal. We were a mixed bowl of veggies, protein, and carbs. I may have bought my dress at a second-hand store and yours came from Rodeo Drive; you can't tell in the dining room. Now we are allowing division to separate us into classes based on financial ability. I think the classes should be based on intelligence, common sense, and knowing what is right.

I have yet to finish the new book in my life, The Bible, but I know what my moral compass tells me. Having pleasure while someone is suffering is not something I can do. I would never do that. I wouldn't consider it. You don't have to go to church or have God to know what is right or what is wrong. Feeling you are significant is wrong. Thinking you are better than anybody else is wrong.

We are all born naked. As spirit enters the body, our skin bag is now complete. We are body mind and spirit. That is who we are. I don't care how many jewels you stick on your forehead; you are still merely a skin bag with a spirit inside. ***When you realize this is all you are that you came here to be something special, but not important. It might change your vision of what you see in that mirror.***

I was able to have the same chances as everybody else to be in the front row at a show. And now I wouldn't even think about going. I do not want to be where we are divided based on what we can afford. And what our priorities are. I think it's a sad world we have become.

Because of what has happened in this world over the last decade, the simple life that you and I knew ten years ago, many will never get to experience. The sad thing is, we created this reality.

My grandpa was right. Man is ruining his own nest.

CHAPTER 22
MAN IS RUINING HIS OWN NEST

I've met many new friends on this journey. One friend commented on one of my YouTube videos. I suggested he reach out privately. We have been friends ever since. This email he sent at the perfect time.

This email from my friend wraps up the first half of this book. It's about to get raw, emotional, hard, and real. I cannot be sorry. I was where you are. I am no longer there. I can show you the way out. Do not blame yourself or feel guilty. You are where you are at this moment. At this moment you can decide to go another direction. Yesterday does not matter. There is only this moment right now. What do you have to lose?

Cari. I'm just now reading down through this email that you sent me back then. I'm sorry if I did not respond to it. Whatever you had going on with this guy, I cannot go there. As you know, I am a watchstander. I look all around this world because I've been all around it. And I have seen many good things.

The way I see it, good ones outnumber negative ones. But the negative ones are louder. They seem to carry more clout. And they continue to come after me up here on my mountain. I guess this is that duality that you all talk about. At times, it gets so overwhelming that I just want to take cover. And I do that.

But this gets tiring. The mainstream media keeps throwing all this s*** out at us, that which they create. People's minds get polluted. These men that you know, it seems that they come at you. God knows, all this hell I've been talking to you about since I've known you. And I'm sorry for some of the things that I have said. Our world is in a pretty bad place right now. I think that is pretty obvious to most of us. Those of us who have grown older, have come to see this.

Now we have Congress talking about things that they can barely even understand. We see those who are standing up and denying all of it. These things that do not fit into their paradigm. This stuff does not fit into the way they want to rule our world.

Where I am now, I find myself dealing with narrow-minded individuals. These ones who have been stuck up here on this mountain, knowing nothing more than what they see right in front of them. Having no clue that there is so much more out there. That it has to be.

I see some of the stuff that you are posting. And I can see that it is not easy. I can read between the lines. I remain silent. I do not want to get wrapped up with all of those others. I got too much going on right here.

I will say that I keep hearing more and more about this place where you are now. You are there where you need to be now. Mount Shasta. And yes, if there was a way that I could stand up for you. I would do so if there was a way. But for now, you go girl.

Rock & Roll.

PART TWO

You must let go of everything. Nothing can matter. If you let anything matter, you are plugged into something that you should not be plugged into. It is not necessary. The small stuff is all there is. Enjoy it.

CHAPTER 23
RESPECT

The way white man acts towards the Native American is, "We gave you land. Shut up. Be happy."

The thing is, they are the ones who know how to take care of this land. We came in and bulldozed it. We planted grass and palm trees in the desert and paved the parks.

Then we take Hawaii in the game of politics. We are white men who came from Europe. We have no business in Hawaii. There you bulldoze and build resorts and golf courses. We deliver white man to trample on your land. The man who has no respect for your culture whatsoever.

I believe to visit Hawaii; you should have an understanding of the land and respect for its culture. It is not America. To live there, you must take a course to learn the culture, learn the language and alphabet.

Do you have any idea how many rocks are sent back General Delivery to the Post Office? People don't realize it's not a good idea to take a rock from Haleakala. When "bad luck" strikes, they send the rocks back.

To keep the land protected from further damage, people need to know why the land is sacred and how to keep it that way. They need to know what they can do to protect it.

I say we let Hawaii be Hawaii again. We have no business there. Let's let them have their island back before we turn them into another America. Why do we have this need to "take over" or "own" everything?

First, we take over Native American land. Then we Americanize Hawaii. Now, we've targeted another island, and more humans to screw. We have gone too far. You are saying it is okay for power and money to trample the human beings on this planet who don't have power and money.

This is not okay with me.

CHAPTER 24
PURPLE PEOPLE UPDATE

Checking back in on our light purple couple with the child now getting some form of education. What is happening to this kid? To keep it in touch with its royalness, they are allowing this child to run the household. Seeing what makes this animal tick amazes the parents. They cannot believe the weirdness and oddness of the decisions this thing makes. It is doing things they would never even consider doing.

It is nothing like them. But they are allowing it the grace to discover its way. Befuddled and confused, they keep it fed, warm, and alive. Safety is not something they can help with any longer. This child has no fears, let alone of heights. He is swinging from branches like monkeys.

The birth child they gave up spends all of its time in boarding school. It is being scrubbed and polished and taught which fork is used for what. They must know the rules of etiquette. What an embarrassment it would be if a child picked up the wrong fork at a gathering of other "important" people.

They have the library at their disposal and are expected to read all of the books on the left side by a certain age. They need to sound brilliant. They need to speak eloquently andact ike they know what is important. Even if they are faking it.

CHAPTER 25
UNTANGLING BACKWARDS BELIEFS

Isolation. Animals don't and can't disappoint. There is just love all around my space. Even down to the neighbor dog who prayed. I was sent to his rescue. All I do is plant seeds. Then my work is done. His spends a whole lot more time with him. He is showing that huge chocolate lab that yes, you are loved and deserve to be loved. The energy has shifted. I feel gratitude from that big bundle of love with the tight shock collar.

Daily, I am visited by about a dozen squirrels, two little squirrels (not chipmunks, not sure – feisty little dudes), two sets of crows (monogamous for life – we aren't supposed to be), and Steller's Jay.

The squirrels climb up on my wooden storage board to poke their head in the window. I feel like I have trick-or-treaters daily. They are so cute. They can get a little insistent. When three come at once, you have to know the drill. You can't give one a peanut. You must give three at once. If one gets a peanut before the others, they don't see me with a peanut for them, they see Larry with something they want and they go after him. It is fun to watch how we are naturally, without the programming.

When I see a squirrel standing before me, and I throw a peanut right at him, he can't find it. His eyes are on the sides of his head. If I hit him, he can find it. It is beautiful to see these creatures running all over the tall trees, and then jumping to a cable. Not seeing directly in front of them, these little things scale a high wire at full speed without missing a step.

This is the difference between you and an animal. They have never been told they can't do something.

Every day of my conscious life, I have been a seeker. Turning over every rock, flipping over every leaf, I have been searching for clues. Unsettled. On a quest to a mysterious place that I know I have to find, yet it is not something of this earth. What was I looking for?

Going on eight years ago, everything changed for me. I appeared before someone who had been waiting for me. I was finally ready to know the answers to life's questions. Once we made the connection, the lid to Pandora's Box flew open, never to close again. Once you find this path, and you allow it, the path takes over.

Somewhere in the last four years, I realized I was no longer searching. I was there. I found my way home.

There is a destination. There is a place you want to "end up" as your goal while you are walking on this rock. For all of the friends I had along the way, they know what I am talking about. I had a lifetime of friends.

I had friends at every level of my consciousness. Every single one of them, I elevated away from. Friends didn't ever leave me. I was pulled through every single relationship. I couldn't stay anywhere for too long or I wouldn't be here to write this book.

That is the way life works. We have become lost sheep and none of you know which way to turn. You are so lost that you don't even know you're lost. You turn toward the pretty people with nice clothes on TV. They must know something, or the cameras wouldn't always be on them. You stay stuck to your screens to see what the next thing is that will unfold to further confirm, yes, we are all going to hell in a handbasket.

You know in order to keep on top of what is going on around you, and places you've never imagined going, you must see the story. You have no idea that the more time you are engaged in the story, the deeper and more involved the story will get. You know you are not the only one giving this story energy. There are zillions of you out there heavily emotional about what is going on - because of the energy you are giving to it. I wrote another book about this in great detail.

This book is urgent and it has a purpose. This book is going to be the bridge to bring you back to where you want to go. This bridge will remind you of who you are and why you came to this rock in the first place.

You know a big part of your private insides, the interior castle you cannot share with anyone else, it is yearning for you to know why you are here. The world you have been placed in feels so foreign to the world you see yourself in. But there is no way you can be in that world because this is the world where you "ended up." This is the world you believe you were to be born into. It is the role you were destined to play.

This is what you believe.

Every family has that "black sheep." That horrible child the entire town talks about because they left the family and the _____. How dare they? It was their birthright. It was their responsibility. They were next in line.

We are so backward.

This book will explain how you are not what you were born into. I will go back a little to bring you forward. You need to see what was placed before my eyes to see. I have seen something that explains who we are and how we got here. I knew it, but I haven't had the words to express it. As of two days ago, all of the answers came through.

I was sent to Maui on August 6th, two days before the fires. I was in Kihei, looking at Lahaina as the fires started. I witnessed and experienced the heaviness of the island. I witnessed what Hawaiians can do. They are self-contained. I witnessed what white man has done and continues to do to the island and to the people. I was there for ten days.

I never "think" about why I do anything. I know the answer always comes. Why I was sent to Hawaii seven months ago became crystal clear.

Two days ago, I woke up at 5 AM, crying and shaking violently. I saw why I was sent to the island. Everything now ties together. It makes everything make sense.

I was told to get in the hot tub in the snow at 5:30 am. It was magnificent.

You may or may not know that I've written four books, the first is in production right now. I have another book that

I am releasing one day that I wrote in 2017. I have many books that will come from all the dictation I do every single day.

The most important book I will write is this. It has not been written yet. It is coming through me right now. I had to be shown my Maui experience to tie it all together. It is powerful. It is painful. It is going to shake up the planet. I hope to God, it pisses you off. If it doesn't, you are the problem.

You can't believe who I am, yet you can't do what I did to get here. You can't know if it is real or not. It's got you so curious. To you, I am a nut case. I'm full of surprises. You don't see half of them.

You've heard of people who channel entities such as Lee Carol, Esther Hicks, and Paul Selig, too many to list, and many who haven't come out. You guys certainly don't make it easy to be a light worker on this planet.

After meeting Alden in Sedona weeks before he died, my connection to Source was restored. I now channel information as well, I just don't have "one" entity. I have a panel.

I've spent years in silence. I don't have conversations with people. I don't talk on the phone. No partner, no animals, no friends, no hanging out. I am completely unplugged from everything outside of myself. I give nothing else my energy or attention. That is how I got here. Absolutely nothing matters to me. Everything is exactly as it should be.

The other book being published right now, *Becoming Immaculate*, was not written for the general public. It was written to wake up the ascended masters who have flocks; the spiritual and consciousness teachers. Their flocks are clinging to them and listening to their every word. They are counting on them to show them the way.

It is for the ascended masters, but it is a step-by-step process of how I became what I am. The book is my life story and I openly share everything. I am an open book. I have an immaculate memory. If I wasn't sure about the details, I wouldn't put them. That's not how I roll.

I do not attach to any leader or guru. I found my own path. I have been pulled through my path at lightning speed in order to do the work I am doing. I was separated from my entire existence on this planet to do this work. I speak to no one. I live alone and I am isolated. The only people I talk to have four legs and I feed them peanuts.

The first chapter of the book explains how I represent a panel from the other side. By becoming an empty flash drive, a blank canvas, many are with me as I walk the planet. I am open eyes, ears, and all of the senses. I am taken where I need to go. I am the voice that asks the questions. I see things that you cannot see - even though we are in the same space. That is why I am the device used for the work I do. This is why I'm always silent and alone. I am needed desperately. I am always the last to know, but the first to go.

Because I know I'm going to be on my computer, writing all day, I have been given the most beautiful, glorious blanket of snow, and it is still snowing. God knows the conditions I like. He never disappoints.

I recently had to walk away from the only connection I had here in town. I realized I cannot have any friendships. When I finally unplugged from every last thing that had any circuit connected to me, that is when this final experience was able to unfold. I had to be completely solo.

CHAPTER 26
THE PANEL CHANNEL

When I was in Maui and the island was burning, vacationers were asked if they would leave the island. It was also requested to cancel your plans if you were heading to Maui. All resources were needed for the islanders. It happened. It looked like Seattle after 911. I remember driving to KMPS on the morning of 9/11 as the show had to go on. I had to be at the station as the reality of our new existence unfolded. No cars on the road and no airplanes in the sky as I passed by two Seattle airports. It was creepily eerie.

How wrong would it be that people are out partying, paddle boarding, parasailing, and having fun when there are people down the road suffering and dying? That could never be okay with us as humans. We would never say okay to this, right? So, people left the island. It was good. It was respectful It was a powerful message. Humans were leaving the Islanders to do what they needed to do until the government stuck its face in it again.

I'm trying to understand this. The island was burning. People were asked to leave out of respect. And they did. We did not want to be there. We could not be with friends or family having fun while others were suffering. This is so confusing to me.

Man is ruining his own nest post:

I now know why I was sent to Maui. Two days before the fire. It all makes sense. I know you like to laugh at my expense, and I don't care, because I know who I am. You are so curious; you can't figure me out. Here's the deal. You've heard of channels like Paul Selig, Lee Carroll, and Hicks, there are many people who channel others. On the road to my enlightenment, awakening, whatever label you would like to attach to it, I was brought to meet my higher self in a capacity I didn't know was possible. I got to drop every part of Cari, the human, and connect completely to my higher self. I erased all of the human story, the emotion attached to it, and everything along the way. I fly completely solo. I don't speak to people.

You can't do that. That's why you cannot fathom who I am.

In the process, I met Alden, and he is part of my panel. My higher self is on the panel. God is on the panel. There are many on the panel. My grandfather popped in on the panel. There are more than two voices coming from me. I am boots on the ground for many.

Alden is the joker of the group. Today after I knew to post about the panel, he gave it a name. The Panel Channel.

I am the one who cleaned my slate, and emptied my flash drive, so they could find me. They needed me. They have sent me out to see things you cannot see. I now know why I was sent to Maui. And I'm writing about it now. You have not seen this side of me.

Yes, I have a book coming out telling you all about how I went from a normal operating human to what I am today. It is step-by-step. It is what I did. To me it is simple. If you do what I did, you too, will be enlightened. When you're here, you will know why we are here. You don't care if anybody's laughing at you. You know you know.

The book I wrote is not for many people. It has been written for enlightened masters, for the masters of the spiritual consciousness game to take the final steps to wake up. They need to bring their flock to the truth. The truth is so far away from your reality You cannot comprehend it. The book being published right now is the story of my transformation. This new book I am writing was inspired by something my grandpa said when I was very young. And it's going to be the title of this book. Man is ruining his own nest.

CHAPTER 27
WWJD

What is the bottom line; what am I saying? If you look around you, you realize the world seems seriously disturbed. Not a lot of direction, nobody knows what to do. You believe the way to get answers is to hear from the guy who was here 2000 years ago. He has no concept of the reality you have created for yourself. He would never have agreed with this; he'd be shaking his head.

This is why he has not shown up again. Actually, that's not the only reason. Why would he come? You would not hear him if he did. He would not be the correct "TV" version of Jesus that you can buy into. You wouldn't be able to believe it if he did show up, no matter what form he took. You prove this day in and out. I have an example.

A neighbor in Newport had the chance to have his prayers answered. Let's just say when the chance is right there before you, you really don't want them.

I will call him Larry. I offered Larry the rocks in my front yard. I was done. I was pouring concrete. I sent an email and then I never looked back to see if he responded. He did. The next day, Larry was stoked to know he had a bunch of free rock as he had his yard guy coming over. He responded via email, and he knocked at my door. I wasn't around apparently.

It ended up he got his own rock, but we had a good conversation. We were talking about a few "landscape" related things. He came back to me with, "If I had a list of the five people I would want to talk to, dead or alive, ____ would be number two." Some lady, I have no idea who she was – horticulture expert I believe. Of course, he baited me. I said, "Who is number one?" This is when he didn't know who he was dealing with; he gave me the whole list.

Number one on the list was the guy from Jerusalem. Number five on the list was Nicola Tesla. At that time, I wasn't nearly as advanced as I am now. I didn't have any personal connections to anyone on his list. But I knew people who did. My friend Maria Elena already channeled Jesus, prior to hearing from "The Big Guy."

You will be introduced to Chad Andrews who runs the Ascension Chamber in Phoenix in my book about Sedona. Chad brought the chamber to life by channeling Tesla. I had Larry covered with two of the people on his top five list.

This was when I learned the truth about y'all. You "say" you want to have your questions answered, but when push comes to shove, and you have answers staring in your face, you find that you really don't want them.

When I went back to Larry and told him his life had just become a dream come true, he couldn't get away from me fast enough.

All you have here is the world you created, the world you were told was yours. I'm telling you the world we have is messed up. If we want to fix the problem, we have to take a very big step backward to see the problem. You cannot see the problem when you are part of the problem.

You cannot see the problem when you are part of it, yet you are denying that you have anything to do with it. In your eyes, your hands are clean. Incorrect. Every human on this planet has had a hand in saying 'yes' to what you are looking at. Every human on this planet needs to have a hand in saying, 'Let's fix this.' Let's do what's right. What is right?

In a perfect world, every human would be born and encouraged to become who they are. They would not be influenced by elders, parents, or others. Everyone would know that the child is on its own individualized, customized, and personally planned path. Knowing this frees you up to know that *you are on a very individualized, customized, personal path that you designed*. If we all gave ourselves the space to be who we are, we would find our way to what we came here to do.

Find our way to that space as if we all agree to it. Because of the systems we have in place, many of you will take a very long time to even begin thinking about walking down the stairs. You think you like how it feels being in the glass castle. But you know it doesn't feel good. It can't. You are not being who you are. Yes, you may look amazing and speak eloquently. But this is not who you came here to be. This didn't exist until we created it. No one on the other side came here to become rich and powerful and run the world. It is not the goal. It is never why we come here. We certainly blow ourselves up enough to believe it.

We come here to find a way to our soul. To our truth. We come here to put ourselves through lessons. We want to graduate from them and move beyond the lessons so we can go through another lesson and then another. We want to keep moving as we are fluid. We are not to stay stuck. We are not to be in one place with just one person.

We've decided we need to own each other. The fact that we have contracts and refer to people who do not follow the contract to a "T" as a cheater. Cheating is when somebody does not do what the contract says. Marital or otherwise. We are not here to be locked into any reality. We are to be fluid. We are to be forward-moving always. When you are "cheated" on, you just become a victim. Take the lead. Stop giving it away. No one can "cheat" on anyone. You can cheat at poker, but you cannot cheat at thoughts. They are there. You just can't say them. We must follow our plan. Most of the time we don't have the balls to say what needs to be said. Rather, we hurt each other. It is easier than telling the truth for some wild reason.

We need to throw out our contracts. We need to throw out anything that binds us to something that we know is not who we are. It may be you for that particular moment, but it's *Paradise by the Dashboard Light*. You're praying for the end of time to end your life because it is not what you hoped it would be. And you "promised" you would be there till the end of time.

You can die with that person that you grew up with and that you promised to love forever. Or, listen to the part of you that is dying to explore who you are. I am not saying to walk away from your high school sweetheart. I am saying encourage each other to go find that part of yourselves that you have yet to find. Give each other the grace and space to explore who you are and what you've been missing. It is only then that you can come back together when you allow yourselves to become who you are. You cannot know what happens next, but you cannot know regardless. Why not?

We will not be involved nor care at all about the stuff going on because we are happy with ourselves. When you are happy internally, what is going on outside cannot affect you. Your love and light are all you need to shine. Shining your light helps take care of the outside world.

I can't bring everybody forward. But you can. We need to love ourselves and we need to help others learn how to love themselves. It's a very private journey. You could do every single bit of this without saying another word to another soul. But you have to find a way to unplug. You have to disconnect from everything you are plugged into outside of yourself.

The trick is just once to push yourself outside of your comfort zone. Do something that is so out of your reality that it will blow you away. Stretch yourself. You don't have to tell anyone. It is not elastic. It does not return to its original shape. Every time you push yourself beyond this space, you have stretched your personal boundaries. You said, "I am capable. Look what I can do. Oh my I can keep doing more." You will find that you are an unlimited being.

We are flailing because we don't have anyone to look up to as our leader. Religious leaders represent God, you know you can't look at them. Political leaders; don't even get me started. We need to revisit how this planet functions. The stars are out of alignment.

As far back as we can remember, we were taught by example and by every other human to find a partner, get married, have kids, clock in, clock out, retire, die, rinse, repeat.

I'm not sure what part about that seems attractive to you, but that is not why we are here.

For any new baby born onto this planet, the best thing you can do to give them a head start is to let them be who they are. Keep them safe, and keep them fed, but let them gravitate to what interests them. Keep them safe and keep yourself sane by not letting them walk all over you. You are allowed to have boundaries. Speak to them as the soul that they are. Don't speak to them as a toddler or a child. You need your space your way, while they need their space theirs. You give them theirs and they give you yours.

Encourage them to find what makes them tick. Allow them to follow that cord. That cord takes them to what they need to know. It also takes them to the people we need to meet along the way to get to "it."

We find our personal villages. People with the same interests, skills, and abilities that we bring to the party. What I bring to the party is nothing that you bring to the party. We can all be on the same ground, share our experiences, and what we know how to do, and make a very beautiful and balanced planet. We will have many lovers; we will have many babies. We are here to populate and re-create and make this world into something magnificent.

At this rate, there will be ash, rubble, and piles of burning buildings everywhere, and soon. We will be back to starting over again and seeing if we can get it right, yet again. What is it going to take? How stupid do we need to be? Pretty damn stupid as far as you're showing so far. How have we become a society attracted to wealth, power, and money?

You all have a Bible that was written over 2000 years ago. The Bible is very clear, and it was written in ancient times. But you have been hearing the translation from ministers and preachers for centuries. Internalizing the Bible as a human is a challenge. How do you think it would've been written by God or Jesus today? Would they love what you have done to this planet? Would they see you as being Christlike? Go ahead, judge yourself. I will give you a minute.

I cannot judge. I have been you. I know how bad it felt to be me. We come here to feel those feelings. Allow yourself the grace.

We listened to Buddha, and we still carry his messages today. We listened to Jesus and some of you still carry his messages today. Many of you are sitting back and waiting for him to come back to fix everything. How many lifetimes are you going to wait? Can you see a man in a white robe walking across a valley getting to you anytime soon? Where exactly would this valley be?

Rather than waiting for miracles to come and save you and "fix" things, reach inside for your moral compass and lend a hand. You know that is what Jesus and Buddha would do. They would go to their interior castle knowing the world has gone mad. It is the only way to find the way out; to go within. There you will find a way to fix and improve everything. It is waiting for you to listen. You cannot fix things by looking at them or giving them energy. Look away. There you will find the answers.

Assume no one is coming. You pretty much know the state of the world. Unless we all see a big spaceship dropping someone "new" off, not one special soul is going to emerge like the Wizard of Oz. No one is coming to give us faith and tell us what we need to do. Honey, we are all there is. You need to find faith within yourself because you came here with a plan. You came here with a reason for being born. We truly must do this alone. We are all we have.

On the other side, before we come to "human," we come from a space of love. Love is all we know. We don't feel anything "icky." We step into human form to experience what it is like to "feel" the gamut of human emotions. We do not come here to program ourselves to not experience these emotions. We want to experience feelings and growth. Expansion is why we come here. Not to be buried deeply in a story that is impossible to get out of. When we don't feel good, we know we are not on our path. When we feel good inside, we know we are. If we used our own personal feelings as our own barometer and only followed good feelings, this world would be happy and there would not be war. There would not be unrest.

People would be so involved with sharing the love they have by finding their path, that they won't want to look at the icky stuff you are creating over there. Only the people who are miserable and have not found their truth are involved in the icky stuff over there. They give it energy. They feed the monster. If you're happy in your life, you do not have time nor would you waste your personal energy inventory on things outside of your reality. You would only deal with things where you felt comfortable.

Anger is the stupidest thing I've ever heard. Most of you are angry, sitting with your phones on your couch. You're not going over there to do anything. You're just mad at everything. Either go over there and take action or get over it.

Do you like that feeling?

Then stop it. Stop looking at everything going on out there and take responsibility for the only one who can do anything about it. Stop looking outside of yourself and feeding anything going on that you cannot control. Be silent. Get away from humans and go to nature. Shut up and listen. You will hear everything you have been waiting to hear

Remember those days when you grabbed random props to pretend? Our parents saw us pretending. People around us saw us pretending. You know they told you what was and was not acceptable in their world with your pretend games. You started feeling shame, so you had to pretend in private. Soon, you forgot you had a fantasy life. It's not burned. It's still the thing that fires your soul. And it's there for you. That baby is wide open and ripe for the taking. Let that fire burn. It will do the work for you. You can be what you came here to be. What they said is a lie. They cannot know who you are. No one can know who you came here to be, but you.

Not even your mother, or your dog.

CHAPTER 28
YOU ARE THE PROBLEM

In trying to describe how you go from being born to where I am without a whole lot of confusion in between, you can't grasp it.

My spiritual books will help explain the mechanics behind this, I'm just going to tell you how it works. Because it is real. It is a thing. If you haven't heard about the law of attraction, I suggest you look deeply into it. It is the law of everything. It is the law of reality. Yet it's a language and a lifestyle most of us can't even fathom speaking, let alone realize it is how we make life happen. We can't fathom that when we believe it, we see it. But more keeps coming.

Using me as an example. I was born with no assistance, and no predetermined path by my family, I was a free agent. By being a free agent, I flailed. I flopped. But I had a clean canvas to work with the entire time. Yes, I had a lot of stories that unfolded and clouded that canvas, but that canvas was still mine to create whatever I desired. That is my canvas.

That canvas brought me through 26 moves and five dads by sixth grade. Lessons galore. Shock that I have not been killed by some of the stupid things I did on my journey. Very shocked that I wasn't arrested. I can't wait to share the story. It is proof that there are angels everywhere. I've had angels watching out for me my entire life. At 21 years old everything would've been different based on one man's decision. I thank you to this day, sir.

For my entire life, I have followed a very distinct gut instinct. My life has been spared many times because of it. This knowing has also taken me to a path filled with magic. I have followed my instinct, that internal movement my entire life. And when I realized that was all there really was, when I fully surrendered to it, my life became beyond magical. There are no human words that can describe life when you fully surrender and allow your course to appear. There's no feeling like it. Knowing that you own your existence completely. There's not another soul on the planet that can knock you down from your bliss. They cannot do it. They are not capable. You can't be budged because you built this foundation. And nobody can knock it down. You are solid. You are the badass pig in the brick house.

Here's how others are raised. This is why it is so confusing to us.

When you're a little kid and you hear all of the things that your life is going to unfold to be, you look forward to them. You hear about the country club. The tennis courts. The parties. The uniforms. The celebrations. There is so much to look forward to in your world.

You are also told about your responsibilities. You are encouraged to get through potty training quickly so you can go to that preschool they had you registered for before you were born. Many of you know you're going to have 17 years of school ahead of you. Not counting preschool. That's the minimum requirement for your family. Your résumé must reflect the family image. We cannot have a black sheep in our midst.

There's the family farm. There's the family business. There are so many family situations that require you to grow up and participate in the family way. It's expected of you. People have lots of babies for lots of reasons. Sometimes it's to run a business.

When this is placed on your plate at a young age, what can you do? It is tragic when at three, little Johnny is learning how to use a tractor. At seven, he is expected to plow the north fields. We all know what fifteen looks like.

I'll use those rich kids again that we've all grown to know, Donald, Jr. and Ivanka. When they were born, their life was laid out for them. There were plans, responsibilities, and expectations. This is your job if you are going to be in this family. You don't have a choice. Even if you suck at it. Put on a designer suit. Go to work. This is who you are.

For me to find my way to my awakening, I had to leave a life of comfort and financial stability. I was with my ex for 28 years. We were very comfortable. We could travel and buy what we needed. Life was easy. To walk away from this "cozy" life, I knew I had to step off of a ledge.

It was a very familiar ledge for me. I was poor my entire childhood. I lived paycheck to paycheck. I knew if I could afford something or not. I had bad enough experience as a young adult with bill collectors to know how important it is to take care of what is important. If you can't afford it, you don't buy it. Being plugged into something like bad credit and bill collectors will quickly throw you down a rabbit hole of despair. Doing smart things feels much better.

After I walked away from a life of comfort and security, I found my way back to me. It really did not take long. Somewhere in all of my writing, I wrote a story about going back to my blue-collar roots. And now I live in Mount Shasta where my uniform is blue jeans and flannel. I am at home. I do not dress to impress. We have uniforms where we live based on what we need and what we're doing. I'm hauling wood months out of the year. Nothing matters to me. I am so at peace with every part of my reality. As I am dictating this, I am sitting in front of my fire looking at Mount Shasta at sunrise. You can't imagine how good it is to be me. But I want you to have this opportunity.

I'm trying to convey this message to those of you in the ivory towers. I'm trying to reach those of you who don't have a clue who you are. There are parts of you constantly peeking through, but everything in your reality tells you - you cannot go there. You live in such internal conflict. On the outside, you look amazing. Everyone would die to be you. But you would die to be them and you can't.

I'm here to tell you that you can. The Puffy Guy was your dad, and you are the Power Baby. You were told what to do your entire life. All you can possibly know is what you've been told. You do know at the deepest parts of your soul who you want to be; huge parts of you are not being expressed. There isn't even allowed to be an uttered thought that anyone can hear. You are not allowed to be what you are because it is shameful. It is whatever Fill in the blank.

People in the tower judge others because they are not _____. They are not filling in the blanks because they don't want to. All of those things we've created; high society, style, fashion, designers, things that even God couldn't buy, you want these things to coif your bodies. You want to look like those people who are getting paid to be seen in public because of people like you.

We were born naked. We were not born with a diamond or a piece of gold or plastic lodged in our forehead to determine our class. We are all just babies, skin bags, and bones. There is nothing different about us. The difference is created the moment we are handed over to you. We are told what we will be, and so we assume our duties.

I am releasing you from your role. Everyone gets a "do-over." This book is your free pass. A "Get out of hell free" card.

People have not understood this and it is blatantly clear. We are born to follow our arrow. We step into the stories, these magnificent mansions we get to reside in for our entire life if we choose to accept this role. But we don't have to. We are not limited to what we are told to do.

As a matter of fact, that is the one thing that we need to change on this planet. Each one of us comes here with our plan. Our path. Our passion. The thing we are here to create, produce, and share with this planet. It is a natural gift that we know how to give. Because so much shit has been piled on top of our brains. We cannot access it. We have feelings about it that stir and make us sad, but we have no idea what it is. We are so covered with the bullshit that's been dumped upon us that we can't find our way out. You are the inner core of the onion that cannot be reached until all of the other layers have been pulled back.

You need to get away from technology, television, news, people, and your reality. You need to get to nature. You need to be just one with you, animals, birds, mountains, ocean. Whatever stirs your soul, go to it. You can't afford not to. I don't care if you need to take out a line of credit on your home; get the hell away from your reality. You have to get away.

Another little nugget you might not be aware of, but if you go back twenty years in time, you will remember what you looked like without your phone. Go back to that person. Take that person with you. The phone is toxic. It is keeping you stuck and keeping the collective crazy.

And then, once you get away, here is what you have to do.

You have to forgive yourself. You did exactly what you came here to do. You have parents or influencers above you. They had parents and influencers above them. They had parents and influencers above them. You have generational beliefs and experiences piled on top of each other that were handed to you. You were told this is your real reality. And you had to assume it. How could you know not to? You take it all on. We do what we're told. How can we know if we have any other options?

Once you shut up and turn off your mind, the answers will come rushing in. This is why nature is required. You are going to have so many voices racing through your head about all of the things you are doing wrong by even considering putting your needs first. You're going to feel horrible. You're going to bring on disease because you left the family, the business, whatever you need to get away from. If this doesn't scream, "Get away – take time for me!" Then nothing will.

Eckhart Tolle's book, *The Power of Now*, was my ticket to silence. The only moment we have is this moment right now. If you think about your life and who you are, your future, and the consequences of defecting, you cannot get to this space. You must be silent. You must watch the waves. With each one that rolls in, let it wash away your mind. Surrender. Just watch the waves, and see how they are all connected, fluid, and always moving. If you are in the mountains, watch the trees. Watch the tops blow in the wind. Watch the animals, bugs, and bees. Watch the magic you have not seen before. Not through this lens anyway.

When you learn to silence your mind, I promise it can become habitual. I truly have no thought ever. You can get here. Stick with it.

After you practice this in silence, you can find a way to silence yourself even when you're in the middle of a crowd. Just start here.

When we allow ourselves to be silent, it's a practice of gently pushing thoughts away as they enter our minds. If something that needs to go on the grocery list creeps in, quickly jot it down, or gently move it away. Go back to the sound of silence. Waves, wind, The hum of a highway. Focus on nothingness.

You will find that when you get to this silent space, you will start to hear things that do not come from you. How do you know they don't come from you? They are things that would not cross your brain. You would not intentionally ever think of some of the stuff that will come through. It will blow you away. But you will be blown away, and excited. That first thought you get is a nugget. It's a breadcrumb. That is your next step. Just be silent. When you are silent and never in your mind, your path appears right before you.

Your path appears if you don't try to plan it. This is the thing that trips you up every single time. Planning is a no-no. Planning engages the brain and takes us away from allowing.

I will share a story about a dear friend of mine and how I helped her quiet her mind. She is a self-admitted control freak. But I gave her a lesson in how to quickly surrender when she feels herself falling down a rabbit hole.

We were walking through a park. She had a large coffee drink. She put the drink down, and I put my hands on her shoulders. I said to relax, close her eyes, and just breathe slowly.

I said, imagine you are paddling upstream in a little tiny boat. There are boulders and rocks and a mountain to the right side. To the left are hills and trees. She's paddling hard because she needs to get upstream. She has to navigate boulders, holes, and eddies. I could see the look on her face with the emotion of these feelings. The grimace.

Then, I told her to throw her paddles in the water. I told her to lay back in her boat and just breathe allow the current to take the boat it will take her where she needs to go. It always does. It is complete surrender. Stop fighting and allow your natural rhythm to unfold.

The look on her face was replaced by extreme calm. Peace. And knowing that this felt right. This is the way we are to live our lives. The more we try to control and plan, the more we are killing ourselves. She surrendered. She threw her paddles in the water.

She enjoyed that moment. We continued to walk and talk for a while. When I asked her what she did with her paddles, she told me she put them next to her in her boat.

When I fully surrendered and threw my paddles in the water, they went downstream; never to be seen again. I fully surrendered to something so much bigger than me. Oh my God, I can't tell you how magical it is to walk in my shoes. You have to find your way here. Being stuck in a reality that is plastic, diamonds, chrome, pavement, stucco, and concrete is far from reality. The further up your elevator takes you, the harder it can be to step down. You must choose to do it. You can say yes, or no to you at this moment. You are the only one who has to live with you. You can always come back in another life and do this same thing over and over until you get it right. No action, that is the result.

I am here to promise you; you are ready for this. You do not **need** power and money. **You believe you do.** Change your beliefs and your reality changes right along with it. It is just keeping you far away from your truth.

Anyone who goes to church saying, "God is the way," then goes back into the penthouse believing they checked the box is living a lie. You were born into a life, or you chose a life that is not what God intended.

We are supposed to be spread out on flat land. There is abundance in our country. The government doesn't need to "own" all of the land. We need to spread out thin and discover our truth.

We are not to be gathered in cities where we congregate piled on top of each other. What is this saying? Is it your level of financial abundance you are demonstrating when you move higher up in the tower? I know it is the one with the most _____ wins. Why did we decide this was okay?

I don't care how special and wonderful you believe you are, I do not agree with you. We are not here to accumulate stuff, fame, power, or riches. We're here to find our journey. It does not involve nor include a penthouse. It does not involve a Ferrari, yacht, fancy clothes, or a business degree. We have created a reality that is so far from the truth that you cannot find the forest for the trees. You have to get out of the buildings and go to God's country. There are so many beautiful places you have wanted to see. Go. You have no idea how much you need this.

When you go, you must go alone. You must go alone. If you claim (or believe) you can't afford to go where you want to go, then go where you can go. If you have one excuse for why you're not able to do the internal work, you don't want to do it. Stop pretending that you do. You are scared to death of shaking your little apple cart. You would rather do nothing. If this is the case, put this book down and get out of my life.

I'm speaking to those who want to feel good about their reality. I'm speaking to those who want to stop looking at what's going on and getting madder and madder at it. The anger you are creating is what is killing our planet. We are killing each other *by thoughts alone.* Thought is what keeps you in the penthouse. Thought is what can take you out. Collective thought is what creates the madness on our planet. Especially the thought of perpetuating that you believe you are special.

To find peace for a moment attempt to go to individual thought. Remove thoughts about everything happening around the globe that are triggering emotions in you. When we are joining others in thought, we are keeping our anger alive and feeding whatever the thing is that you hate. Your hate is making it stay alive. If you don't think about it, you can no longer hate it. It no longer has power over you.

Collectively you feed the animal and keep it alive. If one at a time we pull our thoughts away from that thing that is killing us – we can change the trajectory of not only our life; but everyone else's as well. When we individually stop hating something, it stops the energy of hate from flowing around us. It brings us back as an individual to light and love.

We need to allow God into the situation. Stop thinking collectively about stuff going on. Start loving ourselves and allow ourselves to raise our physical energy. Hate is an energy you do not want to carry. It is cancer. The more you "think" about something on the planet, the more you take your hard-earned energy and give it away. Think about how you are spending your life. Energy is my only currency. I am very careful how I use it.

I don't watch TV or the news, but my gut tells me the world is in turmoil right now. All souls are being called to rise to the fourth dimension. In order to get to the fourth dimension, you do not build a taller building. That is not where the fourth dimension is. It is right here on this planet where the plants and flowers are. Where the animals act with instinct.

You are an animal. How is your self-preservation instinct working out for you? How can you access your gut information when you are told who you are, and you live in a tower? Whatever your tower looks like. Get out of your tower. Go to nature. Shut up. That part of you that has been dying to get out is right there and has been screaming at you every minute of your life. That part of you that wants to die because it can't come out. This is your moment to release that part of you. This is your moment to say, "I love you." This is your moment to say why you were born is really important.

If at any moment you think, "I can't because _____," you are lying. You are the only thing standing between you and _____. The rest are chicken-shit excuses. Get out of your way. Move over so your life can appear.

When everything is in alignment, when you are finally saying yes to you, it's as if all of your chakras are in exact alignment like planets. Everything tingles, sparkles, and jingles and makes your body feel like lightning is going on all around you. It is the most blissful feeling on the planet.

When you are in alignment with you, it's you the human body that you occupy, and your human-issued five senses all saying "yes" to your higher self. Your higher self, you as a puppet-master is giving you clear direction at all times. When you listen and you "climb on board" to the idea, you feel the magic. That is when you feel to your soul that you are in alignment with you. You are in alignment with your purpose. That is you listening to only one step. Your only next step.

When you find this connection to your higher self, it's as if you wink at each other. It's as if you have finally said hello, and now you know how to listen. You will stay together. You will start paying much more attention to what you have to say.

My marriage was not to last long; we were together for a total of 28 years. The damage was done when he told me he loved me and wanted me in his life, but I had to remain silent as far as my spiritual world was concerned. He couldn't listen to anything I had to say. As a human with feelings, I could not give myself to someone who could not allow every part of me in. That is not fair to me the human. He expected me to be there for him, however he could not be there for me. And he thought this was perfectly acceptable. This was when what was left of my marriage tanked.

But I still stayed. It wasn't until I started saying 'no' to things I naturally did – even if I didn't want to do them. I just went along with life as it always was. I never thought about how it affected my gut. I wasn't checking in with the only one that mattered. My 'yes' was implied until I started saying 'no' out loud.

Look at your life. How many things do you do even if it goes against your grain? Why? Why would you ever allow yourself the space to be what someone else needs you to be? How about the grace to love you first? Aren't you the only one who truly can?

When I started listening to my needs and started saying no, we looked at each other like dogs with our heads cocked. Like "what just happened? You said no." That's when we started falling apart. I didn't do the things we always did anymore. And I felt good to me, finally.

I have stories I have shared as I've lived in a zillion little compartments. It's because it has taken me a lifetime to figure this stuff out. I have been where you are. Never rich, but very comfortable. That is plenty rich for me. I really do not like rich people's energy. It is so icky to me. It makes me feel ill. Yes, you are the people I am talking to. The ones I am pleading within the glass castle. You should come down here where I am and take a look. I think you're going to like it here.

The only obstacle between you and where you want to be is your thoughts. The biggest thought that is keeping you from taking any action is what people think. Judgment. Because you've looked at people and had plenty of nasty thoughts about them. You know what they are capable of. That's why you never make a move.

Peel this back a step. You are all painted ponies on the 753rd floor. Each one of you was born here with an arrow and a plan. Each one of you was in a situation that brought you to be where you are. Family, luck, and hard work. That feeling of 'once I get here, I'll be happy.'

Each one of you was born naked and with nothing. Immediately some of you had the world, while the rest of us still had nothing. Having nothing is the only way to go. Having anything more than your basic needs met is what keeps you plugged into a world that you do not want to be plugged into.

Every single one of you at the core feels the same way. You all know that there's no way in hell your mother or father could've possibly known what drives your bus when you came through the birth canal. They decided for you. But they can't possibly have a clue what fires your belly. Nor do they care. They don't want to know who or what you think you think you are. They already decided who you need to be. That is all they care about.

Where you want to be is not following anyone else's path. We all came here with a very specific plan. I am doing what I came here to do now. I've been doing it for almost 8 years. I found this path almost 8 years ago. The last three years have been the most unbelievable, silent, blissful, magnificent years of my life. Full surrender, asking for clarity, it comes to you.

I didn't have God or religion in my life, and now all I have is something so much greater than me that I had to name it, God. God is the only word that was so far from my reality that I could put on this magnificence I experience every day. Go to that God space. Remember who you are. I promise it will come back to you a lot faster than you can imagine. In my woo-woo books, it is explained. The space is already there. It's just waiting for you to show up.

Each one of you wants to defect and go your own way, but because you're worried about what the other one thinks, you won't leave. I am telling you; you are the one who is paving the path for the rest of them. You are leading the way. The one who starts walking out the door first is their leader. You will have the flock behind you as you exit the ivory towers.

But you won't care as you won't look back. Looking back is keeping your paddles next to you in your boat for security. You don't need anyone outside of you to say it's okay. Say to you, it's okay. The world as you know it will collapse overnight. You touched a domino. You did everyone else a favor. You change every life around you by doing what must be done. You place them at their opening for a blissful future.

When the person reading this book realizes it is time to leave, they will take this book, grab a small bag with a few essentials, and they will walk out the door. When you do, throw away the rearview mirror. Now you know you have much more ahead for you. You know what you are capable of. You are fucking tired of being told what you are supposed to be.

Explaining a bit about how this book moves through me; this book comes through me. This section is hitting me hard so it shuts me down and is brought through my panel. It is hitting as hard as other parts of this book, but this is the way my life happens. I am on my couch in my pajamas dictating. What I am writing comes through me. They are my feelings. Oh yes, I feel this way. But I am channeling the book. It's coming from outside of me.

Because I don't see what's going on in the world. I am able to be an empty canvas. I am already unemotional; I can't have anger. If I did have anger ability, I would be angry at the stupid people who continue to watch the stuff that they hate.

I've been praying for a worldwide blackout to kill electronics for at least a hot minute. I know that's not the way this happens. This was a hard journey for me, but now that I am here, I see how easy it was. The hardest part was how long I stayed stuck in my old stories that didn't feel good. When I was somewhere that didn't feel good, I knew I needed to leave, but I stayed. I stayed in situations for far too long.

I took 5 1/2 years to mourn the loss of my first husband, which should've taken me five minutes. I left him. I stayed in a relationship for 28 years that should've been 10. I don't know. We are where we are. There is no looking back. There is only this moment right now.

This is the moment I have and all of this comes through me. It is for you to realize we can topple those towers overnight if you start following your arrow. It is not about me. Get off of the big fancy golf course and go to the par three course in the small-town next door. Walk the course. See the geese.

Don't dumb your life down. Walk out the door. I did it the hard and very slow way. You already know how you feel inside. Follow your feelings. If you know God, you know you will be provided for. You know everything you need to make you successful on your journey will show up. God did not intend for you to think you are above another man.

I look at money like Monopoly money now. I trust what I need will always appear. Five figures in repairs in January alone. I had repairs in October, November, and December. The repairs were all finished by the day of the first snow event on January 5. Because my life is full of miracles, and I am always provided for. Now that you can allow it, you are provided for. You have a recipe to start your life. You have permission at this moment to get the fuck out.

Because I shut up and followed my arrow, oh, my stars, how the beauty shows up. I followed only one step at a time. You get where you want to go when you only await one step. When you think you should plan two or three steps ahead, you already stepped off of your merry-go-round. When you shut up, the next step shows up.

My trail of breadcrumbs was 78 books that are listed in the back of Season One of the four-book series. It was the trail of books that opened me up to understanding the spiritual world. With the books and my surrender, I ended up here. It is so magical.

CHAPTER 29
PAVING A NEW WAY

Today is a huge vision day. Lots coming through. I woke up to a vision of me kneeling down on a huge piece of land with no end in sight, laying bricks and mortar. I am laying a winding path through a field. One stone at a time that seems to appear before me. I am far away, and the path is long; I'm digging, planting, and sealing something that will last. Very unlike stuff built in the United States. We live for orange cone season.

There's a big fence, but a wide-open gate. One person has to be willing to be the first to put their toe on the line. They all want to. They want to say 'Yes, she's right.' But agree with me and they go against everything that they've been taught. Make that instructed.

Who wants to be the first brave soul to cross that line?

There are many people on this planet stuck with a line in the sand they cannot get beyond. They want somebody to tell them what to do, and that it's all going to be okay. We have no leaders anymore. We felt leadership before. Now we are flailing because we don't know where to look.

I'm here to tell you that you are the leader. You are the one we've been waiting for. You are the strong one. You are the one stuck in a suit that you do not want to wear. I don't care if that's a business suit, a fat suit, a racist suit, whatever suit you are wearing take it off and walk through that gate. Be the second. I was first. I paved the way.

It's a path that is a new way of doing things. There is nobody on the path behind me. Definitely no one ahead of me. There are many people at the gate which is wide open, but nobody wants to be *the first* one to walk through. Many are peeking. I know who you are. I am proud of you for peeking. You need to start the journey. Why do you choose fear and cowardice?

According to every human being I bump into, the ones who share a story about a place they know, the world is crumbling right before your eyes. We have been doing the same things for centuries. There comes a time when you need to reinvent the wheel. The car doesn't need a driver anymore. Change is necessary.

The old way of American voting is old school. Nobody gets involved. Nobody cares. They want to care, but they feel inept because they can't understand the language. You've made it too confusing. But boy do we like to get our panties in a knot over it. We like to scream and get angry and bring on heart attacks for ourselves and those around us. We've gone stark-raving crazy. The things you say!

The simple truth is you planned your life. You planned the stories that you are involved in. Everybody you bumped into in your life was part of your plan. I'm not explaining spirituality in this book. It's in my other stuff.

The bottom line is that you chose this life. You also chose to be born into the family that you were born into. The goal for every single person who is born is to be who they are. To follow their own very personal arrow. No matter what goo they get stuck in, they are to listen to their voice and follow the path. The journey that they created before they were born.

By being born into these situations that seem virtually impossible to walk out of, this tells me you are an advanced soul. You are somebody that is ready for the hard stuff. The easy way is to stay there and do what everybody tells you to do. The hard way is admitting to yourself, "This doesn't feel good" and leave. The truth is, we came here with nothing, and we truly are happier when we have nothing.

When you have too much, it's almost impossible for you to fathom how life could even be imaginable when you have nothing. It's literally the flip of a switch. If you make the decision to say yes to you and allow whatever your natural plan was to unfold, you will be the happiest person on the planet. Next to me, that is.

Once you say yes to you, you find a way to love yourself. Once you love yourself, you find gratitude in the things that make you happy. The things that make you happy are not shiny and don't cost a thing. The things that make you ultimately the happiest you can ever be are waiting for you after you say yes to you.

You did not come here to be a programmed robot. But you are just that. You are doing what you were programmed to do. It's time to pull out that power pack and replace it with your own energy source. Unplug the flash drives. Drive your own bus. Don't let anybody have domain over you ever again.

Once you find the path to you, once you get in your lane, you will never let anybody budge you out of it ever again. You will see what feeling good all the time feels like. You will never let them bump you out of your lane again.

CHAPTER 30
YOU LIVE LIKE CHRIST?

Why do I hate people? The word hate isn't from a hate you recognize. Hate is not an emotion for me. It is the only word that is vile enough for what humans, mostly Americans, have become. The fact that I can see you from my lens, and you say you cannot see what you are doing is disgusting to me. There is no other word for it. How can you not see how you are treating each other? What you are doing to each other.

You love looking back at history and naming names of people that took down thousands of people. It seemed like we all stood by as thousands of lives were lost. How could we be so lost that we allow something or someone with so much power to hurt others? We would never do this, right? We wouldn't join in with the bad guys. We are here for the little guy. The one who can't speak for himself. Is this true?

I can't believe, how much whining I hear about an upcoming election in the United States. I hear people screaming at each other, trying to decide which is the lesser of two evils. How can we come to this? Are we really down to deciding which is the lamest horse?

We learned from Buddha, Jesus, and other wise men. Many people walk on this planet with amazing messages that need to be heard. Sadly, we find a few tiny nuggets and that is all we grasp onto. We swear we are going to live by it and fight for the truth. Then it gets filed away somewhere in our brain.

From my lens, you guys have lost it. What were Jesus's messages? Do unto your brother as you would do to yourself. Love yourself, love your neighbor. Be honest. Don't hurt anyone. Be true. Share. The golden rule. His words have been translated into many languages, and handed to many people at the top of the stairs. It was for them to share with their people translations of words written thousands of years ago.

You say you hold onto these words and you live by them. You say you live like a Christian. Holy cow. Get back to that mirror.

I cannot believe what you have allowed yourself to become. I don't get out much. When I do, it is to hear a certain conversation or to meet somebody, there's always a reason. Always. I am not here to make friends. I am guidance.

I was sent to Maui two days before the fires. The energy was so heavy for those 10 days. I was sent there for a reason. I don't go on vacation. I was sent there for the people, and for the island. Go ahead and roll your eyes. What are you doing?

When I knew my book was done, I knew I was to go on a cruise. I used to love cruising. The last cruise I went on was at the beginning of my awakening. All I remember are the people I was with, the expansion I was going through, and the amazing glaciers in Alaska. Plus, I got upgraded to an obstructed view room from a small indoor cabin. It was magical. It was the last time I went on a cruise ship.

When I heard Norwegian cruise lines had Solo cabins, I knew this was the perfect opportunity. I hate that because I will only travel alone, I have to pay double occupancy. Double occupancy is bullshit. We need to be alone more.

I knew it was time, so I emailed Nick from NCL and told him I wanted to cruise out of LA in early March, in a solo cabin.

He called me back and pretty much said, that's going to be tough Impossible is what he meant. I do know these are sold out long in advance.

We ended up experiencing a miracle together. Out of LA, a solo cabin opened up sailing on March 3. That was less than a week away. I was planning on visiting my daughter if I went to LA, this would pencil out perfectly.

He could not believe the cabin opened up. I laughed and told him this is how my life works. I live in the land of miracles. And then I remembered that morning I wrote a blog post titled *"We Forgot Miracles Exist."* He couldn't believe he was having this conversation with a woman at the end of the line in California. He needed this inspiration. We both got a miracle that day.

I will call all of you out who claim you believe in, and live by God's word. You've gone to church; you've always known what you're supposed to do; to be Christlike. What have you been told? But you're not doing it. Don't you "believe" in God, and trust that your way is already paved for you? It is all about faith, trust, and belief in God. Surrendering to this is what you are supposed to do, right? This is what you know, learning God the conventional way.

My connection with God was very unconventional, and quick. Once the meeting was established, I knew what to do. We no longer "believe" anything in this space. We know. It is downloaded. It is as clear as now.

In the four seasons of my book series, *"Only Beautiful Things Happen to Me"* (#OBTHTM). I give great detail about how my life wasn't working, so I completely surrendered. To what? I had no clue. I spoke to the universe. I completely gave up control of my life and listened to guidance for years.

Now, I merely walk in that space without the need for guidance. I simply "know" what to do, and when. Bottom line, in the boat going upstream scenario, I laid back as my boat turned to flow with the current. I threw my paddles out and they were downstream long before I would be. I fully surrendered.

This book is being written through my lens. I am someone who has been alone for almost 8 years. Alone in the sense of the word that I walked away from every friendship that I ever had. I realized I was in a marriage where he just needed a woman, but he did not want to have a conversation. I got to be completely alone. Being alone takes you places you can't go otherwise. But you can't do it. No one does it.

I have been alone so I could see our planet and life through a lens that nobody has seen. You have no idea what's going on. It might take you five times to read this book before you can identify who you are in the story. But for the love of God, I hope you do.

As I was writing this book, I had a friend for a minute. I knew early on that he couldn't not judge what I sent him. I don't want praise or recognition. I write what I write because it is what I am to write. No one human outside of me can have authority. For a bit, I had to cut that friend off as well.

My best interest is all he has in mind as he worries about what people are going to think. I remind him that I can't care. Nothing matters to me. I am guided, and so I do.

I don't care. I am alone. I am not watching the news. What I am writing is what is coming through me as a human being isolated from the rest of you. These words are coming through because we have lost our way. The path we are to take has been buried under concrete, plastic, glass, gold, and marble. We can't find our way. We are so lost. We can't even see the path.

Without caring what you think, I am writing my thoughts. Frankly, I don't care what anyone thinks. If we cared, we would not be ourselves. That is the problem. We have become a world of functioning robots. Make that 'almost functioning' robots. If you were functioning, part of you would be seeking your truth. You are so lost in your reality that you don't even know you have a truth.

This book is going to help you peel back the layers of the reality that has been created, called your life. A reality with so many layers you don't even know you're living a lie. You are living outside of your reality because you have been programmed. And you don't even know it. That's the part that cracks me up.

CHAPTER 31
MY LEAST FAVORITE THING... POLITICS

First off, watching this planet unfold, I thought we were dumb and dumber. Then, we became stupid and stupider, and just when you think it can't get any crazier, you do another stupid thing. It gets so much more ridiculous that you look around to see where the camera is. Is this seriously, really, happening? Are we doing all of this insanity right in front of each other and we're saying it's okay? I swear I am being punked. This is a big trick and it's on me.

Nope. You've gone crazy.

I really don't know when this madness started. I was living my life in Puyallup, Washington, and my life was starting to go into a tailspin. I was finding answers to the questions I had my entire life. In the meantime, I'm watching a presidential election happen on television.

Before I went to bed that night, I knew history was going to change the next day. Without a doubt. We would either have our first woman president, or by the slightest chance of a minuscule effort, the guy who was on Celebrity Apprentice with his polished children beside him. The guy who loved being in control and power. He could be the president. Either way, I felt a shit show was on the way. And boy, did it deliver.

Growing up, the presidency was a respected position. Looking at what has happened since that election, it is laughable. Even though Clinton had some memorable faux pas, he was still respected as a president. He was just human. And he couldn't get away with it. When you're in the spotlight, everything is in the spotlight.

It was the election between Clinton and Donald Trump when we showed how crazy we are and how much we have lost our minds.

I have been sucked through a vacuum to get to the space where I am because this story has to be shared. We're killing ourselves. And the fact that you guys are all the perpetrators, you're actively killing each other, and you are so blind you cannot see it.

The answers to why you are the way you are is in the pages of this book. I suggest you take the time and read it. I suggest you identify who you are in this book. Because you're going to find yourself in this book. You're going to know exactly when I'm talking to you. Because it's going to rip your fucking heart out. You're going to see who you are and you're going to know that you do not have to be who you are. But you are only who you are. How can you possibly be anything else? Because you are not who you were born to be.

You are who you were told you were going to be. There is a big difference.

I think we are a bit lost.

The biggest problem is because we have no leader. There is not an authority for anybody to look toward to tell us what is going on. At one point, we did look toward the president as the guidance, the leadership, the one who would show the way. We all know now that that is not the case. It is somebody in a polished suit who is a puppet with many many puppeteers behind the podium. We don't actually know, who we are electing. We are electing a big pile of power and money behind any human being running for office. We all know this is how it works today. I don't know how we worked 100 years ago; I don't care. The only time that matters is this time that we are in right now.

What happened? How did we get lost? How do we get back on track?

At one point, we figured we all had one thing in common. It was the fabric that kept us together. That one thing was the belief in something greater than any of us. We called it God. There was a time when God was the answer.

Even during that time, we all twisted and turned God's love and God's guidance into our own expectations and needs. Everything is twisted to serve the man. God is not an entity actually walking around on this planet. He has no needs to be served. We do. Anyone who translates God's word is going to translate it in a way that benefits someone, somewhere. We have to insert our human condition into our translation. Our experience is the only lens we have to broadcast from.

It has been made clear that we need a sprinkle of common sense on this planet. I think we've lost it. I think we're generally going crazy. Our priorities have shifted. Things that matter to you now are ridiculous. You are looking for someone to tell you what is right or what is wrong, and we are flailing. Meanwhile, you are praising and worshipping people with money. We don't know who to ask. You can't go to the confessional and ask the priest. He is a man. He has needs, wants, expectations, and feelings.

Every human being on this planet has something they need. We are all here on a journey. How can anyone be the authority that we go to for answers? We fly around all over the map and in doing so, we give our power away. We give our power to someone else because we don't trust ourselves that our answer is the right answer.

You have got to start spending more time inside, and a lot less time listening to what everybody else is telling you. We've gone to hell. Learning from that fateful election, can we ever learn? I didn't think it could get worse than that. We are going further and further down the toilet. And we know it. We all know it. No one wants to be the first to do anything or say anything.

When I went to bed the night before the election was over between Hillary Clinton and Donald Trump, I knew whatever happened at that point wasn't going to matter anyway. We already rewrote the script of the United States over the last year. We showed we were not the strong, capable powerhouse country that we have been pretending to be.

Talk about showing our true colors and our stupidity. Talk about waving our finger paintings at each other. We've never looked so ridiculous. We let it come down to two of the worst possible presidential candidates on the planet. And we all said it was okay to get to this space. Why didn't we find someone we all could agree on, or at least be able to find peace with?

What you can't understand about people like me is when you hear us talk, you are inspired. You find a glimmer of hope somewhere inside. It doesn't take much with the way your lives are going; this planet is going. Today, I can talk until I'm blue in the face. You have to reach inside to help this rock get back on track.

For those of us living in the United States, we are the most powerful country, right? Isn't that what we thought? Isn't that how we were raised? And now you are literally believing you have no choice but to choose icky or ickier. And you trust that this is your only option. Would you have stayed in line and walked in the showers? You might want to think about this.

We've always trusted that on American soil, we are safe. This is what we always believed. It isn't even the outsiders who are the problem today. It is the secrecy behind the walls of the castles. You can't know what is going on and who is deciding your future. Who is deciding what happens next in your life? Power and money.

The first book I looked into as I started my spiritual journey was the well-known. *A Course in Miracles*. It was definitely not the direction I was supposed to go. But it did lead me to the people I needed to meet. It also taught me language and gave me an understanding of this world people like to joke about. People like me can only come from a place of love and light. We shine light on the path for others. Sometimes we have to play hardball. We do what it takes. We do what we know to do; we never act on our own. It is a directive from something outside of us. The unseen world. We follow our instincts. We are not following the masses.

In my book, I talk about how in a perfect world, Marianne Williamson would be the President of the Federation. Can't someone who can offer up hope and the ability to look for miracles be a better choice than the two you don't want to look at? You "believe" you only have two options. If you weren't aware, all she taught people for decades was *A Course in Miracles*. Don't you think we need one about now?

Your head is in the sand. You're trusting others to show you the way. Are you really comfortable handing over your power? You've certainly done a good job.

Witnessing how politics works from the inside showed me all I needed to see. The party system no longer works, it is antiquated. It can be bought.

In George Washington's days, perhaps it worked. I don't care. We have evolved. It's time to find a new system. One where everybody has a vote, a voice, and a choice. Where everything is transparent. Nothing is hidden behind a platform to support a certain candidate or portion of the population. Every party should support the entire population. There should be individuals running for election and presenting themselves in front of the planet. Not being the 'front man' for an unseen monster we keep feeding.

It's a sad world when even politicians can't explain how their universe works. Politics, taxes, and spirituality; we need to dumb down the lingo. Everyone needs to be able to understand.

The 1700s was a long time ago. Do we really want to keep a system that worked for a small population? We need to snap out of it. We need to reinvent the wheel. The wheel that is rolling down the hill is going fast; it's headed for nails. The tire is flat and the rims are sparking. It has very little to go on.

Someone I once knew well was a politician. I got to see firsthand how you go into politics because you have a passion for something you want to see changed. Your heart and soul are moving forward. Then you get in there. Then you see the power you hold. You see the spinning that takes place. You realize that you can get your name on buildings. You realize that you could be known across the globe if you play your cards right. You find ways to compromise your soul when you never thought you could. You sell out.

My recommendation is that if you want to be in politics and run for public office, you should get one job and it can last six years. This is your chance to make your mark in society. Do it well; give it all you've got, because then you are out. You are fresh blood and new eyes with a vision. You should not be able to run ever again. You time out before your ego steps in. We cannot run this country from ego.

This idea goes namely for the position of president, but one and done. Every person interested in the job should be able to stand before America and explain what they value and show us how they live their life. Let's see their house and how their experience is. Can they run their household? Is everyone happy? We want a president whose household is in order and everyone is happy. We need a leader who we can see through. They must be transparent. Nothing hidden behind the curtain.

Every human being should have the chance to be a leader and express their individuality. We need somebody strong, where we can feel safe and not punked. We want to trust to our core that we picked the right person.

People don't care anymore because they know whatever they want, they have no control. The Donald made a mockery of our elections. Can we trust anything the way it has been done? With the systems currently in place, and all the crap that we've created over the years, it's not working. The right person is not landing in front of us. We don't need a machine. You can't trust a machine.

Many brilliant minds out there. Someone has an idea that can work.

What once worked is not working now. We are flawed. We have two massive machines running this country. Most of the people have no idea how elections work. That is why they sit by, they cry, they pound their fist, they pray. They don't know what to do. It's beyond their comprehension.

They are being represented by a machine and they don't know how it operates. They have a little human standing in front telling them who they are and what they believe in. You are hearing what the machine believes in. They are not allowed to be authentic. If they said what they wanted, the machine would not have them.

You can't know who is running your country. You see a tiny little representative puppet speaking on the dais. What happens when you follow the power and the money? Follow the power and the money and you will know who is running your country. Who is getting rich because this little pony is standing before you taking a human beating? Who is getting richer while you're getting poorer?

Knowing this election was critical, I "leaked" the following chapter on Facebook a while ago. No one will so much as "like" my posts, let alone ever comment. They will agree and tell me in person, but they cannot speak their truth for others to see where they lean. Why are you so afraid to be who you are? Why do you conform to something that you are not? Why pretend to be who you believe they need you to be? I'm pretty sure you will be liked – and enough – being you. Give it a try.

You truly can't have any idea how this works. I am praying to God that y'all are clueless because everything is happening to your world right before your eyes, and you are the creator of all of it. You thinking about it keeps it growing. Think about how many people are "thinking" about it. With each thought about "it," it is a monster receiving fuel. You are feeding and fueling this monster. I don't care what it is.

Since I went into isolation and silence two years ago, I stepped away from any information you are all consumed with. I saw on Facebook long ago that Roe v. Wade was overturned. That was all I needed to see. You people have lost your minds.

As I write this, there is the most important election of your lifetime coming up, and you are all split between what you call, "the lesser of two evils." You are openly and wholeheartedly picking a candidate who is completely despised by half of the country. We're not talking about a slightly icky feeling; we are talking rage, hate, and anger –

by many. These are huge, and dark feelings. These feelings gather people together. Think about what is coming after the next election. It is almost guaranteed. This world as you know it will collapse like Rome. And you are saying yes to it. Think about how angry you will be when your candidate loses. You are so confident that your "love of country" will win over the other guy. To you, this is a horse race with two horses. Have you seen the Kentucky Derby?

What kind of energy are you creating in the USA? I remember as a child this country felt like a powerful place to be. I remember the presidents who stood tall and proud. We looked at them and believed what they said was what they represented. People, all people looked at the flag with respect and love. It meant home. It meant family. It was where you wanted to raise your children. With or without God, it was okay to say the Pledge of Allegiance to your flag. You all knew the words and could loudly belt out, "America, the Beautiful," or "The Star-Spangled Banner." When and how did we forget what this felt like? We were (mostly) proud to be Americans.

Now you know you get a different "feeling" when you see a flag or hear the songs. They represent something different now. Something a little icky.

You know your next step is huge. You know how you feel is telling you to do something that your human universe is telling you otherwise. Who do you believe **you** should listen to? You also know what you do behind a curtain or sealed in the envelope is your little secret, right?

What happened to a powerhouse that was a clear

candidate for all? One that no matter which party represented; they were who they were. They could not fake it. The other party was disappointed, but they didn't want to kill the other people. You guys are raging mad. You are backing your boy so strongly; you should be scared that the other guys are too.

Now you see someone before you spinning their yarn, and you are sucked in like a vacuum. To you, they are the great hope. If they are, how can half of the people in the country despise them? Why are we saying "yes" to this behavior?

We have two lame ducks and you are flipping a coin. How dare you do this to your children? You know you are creating every horror movie you watch and you will be cast as a lead character. I watched "The Handmaid's Tale" from start to finish and truly felt it was your future. I watched "Her" many years ago and knew the same thing. So far, folks, my average is on fire.

The people behind these candidates are the 1% with all of the power and money. You are saying "yes" to letting the powerful and rich push you further into the dirt. You do know your saying "yes" to something you don't wholeheartedly agree with is creating a dirt ball in your body as well, right? It is creating a cancer. It is beginning a dis-ease of some sort because you know you are not doing the right thing. You are doing the thing your _____ expects you to do. It is how you were trained.

Do the right thing. Look further into your options. This is the election that will make America look like the respectable powerhouse we once were. Can you look at the presidential position with the same respect after the *debacles we've experienced? We've seen nothing is set in stone. Every rule can be broken. There is no line in the sand. And anyone can get away with anything.*

In the eyes of other countries, we were powerful and strong. Now you know how they look at us. The behavior you are allowing is a joke. They no longer view America as the respectable leader.

My biggest takeaway is – you cannot believe a word anyone says. The man (so far) in front cannot be trusted that what he is saying is what he means. You know you have to follow the money. The man up front is the puppet. The money and the machine behind him (so far - a man) are what does the moving of parts. Yet you stand idly by and want history to repeat itself. At least I am doing what I know to do. I am writing this (and many) books. Do the right thing.

Look your kids in the eye. Look at what is left of your country and your planet; see what you are handing over to them. How can you explain it to them now so they can be prepared? Are you going to tell them you didn't do anything about it? That is what they see. They don't miss a lick.

PART THREE

GUIDANCE BEGAN AS A MESSAGE

A message came through... "I'm going to be posting a manifesto or something soon. It has been coming out all morning. Make that all day. It's been a ball of dust in my spirit that I knew I had to release at some point soon. It is time. It is longer than I thought. It keeps coming. I say the things nobody else says. I say the things people want to say, but they don't."

CHAPTER 32
PREPLANNED CONSCIOUSNESS EVENTS

It is crazy how I was brought to Maui in early August to be there for the fires. I was there for 10 days. Fast forward to March and I am placed on a cruise ship. The two go hand-in-hand. This is very fascinating to me.

This means preplanned consciousness events were preordained for me with two different events seven months apart. Two different things I had to do, go to, experience, and witness in order to put a puzzle together.

I got to experience contrast, the law of attraction extremes, by two different "vacations." I was there with my eyes, ears, and all my senses. I was there to see what was going on, to feel how it felt, and to know what to do.

This is mind-boggling and fascinating. But I was the receiver, and I was the one who was told where to go, and it all makes sense to me now.

CHAPTER 33
SELF IMPOSED SIGNIFICANT PEOPLE

On the 18th floor of the ship, you entered the special space. The place reserved for people who were born to be special and significant. They were told by mommy and daddy that they are the Power Baby. Mommy and daddy are the Puffy Guy. They are aware they are a special breed; they are definitely special. They are not to communicate with or walk along the riffraff of the middle or lower class. They are to remain in the top 1% on our planet and carry themselves accordingly.

These people get the top few floors of the ship. They have their own suites, their own dining, and their own pool and lounge area. They do not communicate or have to walk their bare feet where ours touched. Those of us on the bottom of the Titanic will never be seen by the people on the 18th floor.

There was a go-kart track and a laser tag experience on the top few floors of my ship. I didn't see them. I never went to the 18th floor because I did not want to experience their energy. I already know what that energy feels like. It is heavy and very dark.

People who think that they are above anyone else truly have a false sense of who they are. They have been trained to be honored and respected at the level of existence they occupy. They truly believe somewhere in their world that those with power and money are better than others.

When I thought about what the collective could do if they wanted to, I laughed when I thought how ironic it would be if it happened. If the people at the bottom of the ship all prayed hard enough, they could flip the ship. For a minute anyway, they would be on the top. Those in the penthouse would be underwater. Thoughts alone can sink a ship. Meaning the people in the penthouse would end up in the basement.

I believe everybody knows we all put our pants on one leg at a time. If we were on a ship that had so much separation as the one I was on, it would be interesting if disaster struck. If we all needed to rally and find strength within our people, I guarantee you the guy or the lady with the big pocketbook and all of the power and money in the world would be the first to try and buy the strength that I carry. I would not give them the time of day. If you believe you are better than someone, you will be learning many lessons that I cannot help you with. We are all the same. You believe you are an improved human version. When you treat someone as you do, you will understand my version of hate.

As a privileged white person, can you ever imagine saying "Yes. I will work for you for the next six months of my life. I will work seven days a week every day to feed people and make sure their lives are simple. This will be my life mission." I don't know one privileged person who would agree to this, but you certainly don't have a problem taking advantage of others.

Growing up in Las Vegas, people came from all over the world to this little town in the middle of nowhere. It was very inexpensive to get there. After I grew up and moved away, it was such an easy place to get back to. It was still so cheap. Flights were nothing. Food was nothing. Parking was nothing. Entertainment was everywhere. Magic was everywhere. It wasn't as vile or disgusting back then.

What Las Vegas became is something I cannot be around. Why did a town like Las Vegas have to change its demographics? I already lived in major metropolitan areas where we had professional sports teams. Never would I imagine Vegas would be this.

The more you bring in, the more you make. It just is about power and money. Isn't that what this entire world is about? That is what we have become. You agree with this. You believe this is our direction. I've got bad news for you.

Large cities. High rises. Cement. Garages. Air conditioning. Not the recipe for success. You will not find your way to happiness in an ivory tower. It is not there for you. It cannot be. You think you're happy. You have all kinds of things tugging at you that say otherwise, but you're told you're in a perfect position. Everybody envies you. They want what you're having. They want the clothes you're wearing. They want the house you're living in. They want your bodyguards. They want your paparazzi team. They want what you have. You look marvelous on the big screen.

It doesn't matter who you are. You know who you are. The one that looks beautiful on the outside. But inside there is something missing. There is a void within you bigger than the Hoover Dam. But you cannot say these words to anybody. Because you have everything. How can you possibly want for something else when you have everything?

But at the same time, you will never walk away from everything. How could you? There you have protection. A safety net. There you will never have to worry about anything. The only thing you would ever have to worry about is if you defect from the family. If you did something other than what you are supposed to be doing in your role as a family member.

I'm sorry, but it sucks to be you. I would hate to be in your shoes. You have no way out. You have no idea there is a way out. You are just going to do this until the end, and you're going to be happy when you get to crossover with all those regrets. You're going to say' dammit I wish I did blank, blank, blank,' but clearly, by then it is too late.

You have this minute. Or you have your next lifetime. Or you have an eternity being stuck with your body because you really don't know what's going to happen to you next. You have all kinds of options. My recommendation, because I know how good this feels; perhaps try leaning in towards doing something for yourself for just a minute. You don't have to tell anybody. It can be just between you and me. We won't say a word. Keep this book under your mattress. If they see it You are a threat.

You are about to discover what it means to have everything; while wanting for nothing. I know you cannot believe this is possible.

When I discovered bookstores in the 1990s, I discovered a self-help section. I truly spent no time in the library growing up.

Reading the backs of some of these books I realized I was not alone. Other people had endured my situation, and they wrote books about it because they got to the other side. They got through their tragedy. This gave me so much hope.

Sometimes, just reading a book from somebody who was where you are, and now they are living a life of bliss makes you think, 'Maybe I'd like to have a little of what they are having.' Even though we seem to be completely happy in Whoville, it's because we are. We don't need stuff. Take our tree, take our roast beast, and we still come from love.

My ex-husband 's philosophy is flawed. You're going to see that it's more than flawed, it's destructive. As a matter of fact, it is downright stupid. It is the worst philosophy anybody has ever come up with.

It's like Larry starting a brand-new job.

Larry walks into the office for his scheduled appointment. He hands over the application. They like him. He goes to his office, sits down, and they give him $5000. He gets paid for showing up. He realizes he doesn't really have to do anything. Sometimes he doesn't even bother showing up - and he still gets paid. He doesn't have to do anything, and he gets paid. He doesn't have to have any skill development whatsoever. He gets money for just being Larry.

He does nothing, he shows up in fancy clothing, and he gets a lot of money.

Having a leg up you step right into the ivory tower. You get to start getting paid just because you are alive. How good can that feel? What is your claim to fame? What are you successful at? What did you do that was your shining moment? How does it feel to have so much without having to do very much? I'm sure that's got to feel really good inside somewhere. I'm not sure where. But somewhere that's got to have a warm, fuzzy feeling.

CHAPTER 34
EARLY CRUISE JOURNAL ENTRIES

I'm not excited, I am numb, but I know this is going to be huge. I have no idea what's going to happen next. But I will find out.

I love my little cabin. I already have my luggage. I feel so at home here. I realize that I am isolated. I'm on a ship with 4700 people. 1700 crewmembers. And I am in my own brutal bubble. I am thrilled. I knew this would be safe and easy for me. I will follow my arrow.

I am now down on another deck in the observation lounge. I saw it from my table, and it looked like a really private and quiet area. Now that I am here all I hear is the rumbling of noise and laughter. I will find my silent places. I already have. I don't have a problem doing that. There may be 4700 people with me on this ship as passengers, but they will not mess with my energy. I am enjoying the rocking of the ship. It feels so delicious.

I realize now that I can be on a ship with 7000 people, and I can be completely isolated. I don't make eye contact with anybody. I don't acknowledge anybody. I am invisible. I'm not really here. Even if they did see me, I am Jessica Rabbit. By the time they see me, I am leaving a trail of dust. I am the fastest walking thing on this boat. No one can keep up with me or even try. I get stuck behind long jams, and when I break free, they always comment about how fast I go.

Thinking about the lives of the people who work on the ship. They aren't like when I first started cruising. They are always on the ship and working every day. But at the end of this cruise, each person on this ship should get some form of a tip, right? When you calculate 4,500 people leaving a tip, they should each get a decent chunk, right? We used to leave tip envelopes or hand them directly to the person. We knew they got the money. Now, who knows what they get? We prepay for tips now. I hope they have a huge bonus to send home to the family in addition to their hourly rate.

I think it has become abundantly clear that I'm going to be doing my retreats, presentations, and seminars on cruise ships. I'm going to do this for the rest of my life. I love being on a boat!

I'm sitting on the cruise ship in the Taste and Savor Restaurants which are on deck seven. I am starting to get the hang of what is where. The front and the back of the ship are so confusing. Accessing my room is so confusing. Once I get close, I'm on fire. I know exactly where I'm going. But I have walked and walked and walked in discovery. It is a blast. Once you realize the fish are always swimming toward the front of the boat, it helps the directionally challenged.

Here I realize that I do need to consume mass quantities of food. As much as I moved yesterday, I was starving. I had a Cobb salad before bed, then inhaled a piece of pound cake from the lounge. You just need fuel for your fire when you burn so much.

Cruise ships have the absolute best food anywhere. They have chefs from all over the world. French onion soup on a buffet line, you would think it would be absolutely disgusting. It was delicious. Perfection. My breakfast was to die for. And I am consuming calories. I'm going to need them.

I am really thrilled that even without the Internet I am able to dictate. This is going to be what I'm doing on this trip. I am pretty fucking stoked about this. I don't need to take my laptop out. I will when I'm supposed to.

It has become abundantly clear that I can be on a ship with this many people, and I can be completely isolated. There are very few people I have cute little conversations with. They are meant to be. They are light, they are enjoyable, and we are meant to bump into each other. Everybody else, I don't even make eye contact.

I am here to be isolated. I get to drive my own bus every day. Eat where I want to eat, whenever I want to eat.

Why do I see seagulls? We are in the middle of the ocean. Did they climb onto the ship?

It feels so delicious to know I could do something like this and be around all of these people with their limited conversations, and they cannot affect me. I can only be affected if I allow myself to engage, and that is virtually impossible. I am not to do small-scale conversational work any longer. My work is more global. I have much bigger fish to fry. The one on one is no longer.

We have a lot more problems on this planet than individual issues.

I need to get an entire wardrobe with the words Zen master. There will never be any questions again. People will see me and see how weird I am, then my apparel will make total sense.

At this point on Monday night, I am really feeling the difference between me and everybody else on this cruise ship. To most people, I am invisible. To many people, I am a curiosity, an anomaly. I don't know who the fuck I am. I just know that I'm sailing into another dimension. I'm ready for it. I am more than ready for it.

I am sitting next to a couple having conversations about what they should order. They are on a cruise ship. They can order any fucking thing they want. But they are discussing it pragmatically about what is right, what is wrong, and what they should share. I am ready to smother them.

Meeting Shelby and Miles was definitely in the cards. We had many powerful conversations. Hopefully, they will hold off on the wedding for a while. But just hearing their conversation over dinner, I knew there was something about them that they needed me. Perhaps the intervention. Perhaps the first couple to listen to me and follow their arrows independently, while still trying to remain a couple. We can't know why people come into our lives. We just know that they do. I just plant seeds. That's the slogan on my website. Changing the world by planting one seed at a time.

I am Jessica Rabbit, and I do not sit still. I don't know how long I have sat in any one place. The longest has been at my dinner just now next to Miles and Shelby. I am on the go nonstop. I don't know where I'm going to end up ever. I just keep going.

I am getting an earful. I am sitting here watching a band doing all the songs we loved from the 70s. This band sounds great. In this group, they were from Cambodia, Jamaica, Asia, Korea, and the Philippines. You name it, they are from there. Not America though. They get the cheapest help to run this ship and they are making millions. It is quite a product.

These workers work their asses off. They are working daily for months and months on end. I'm sure they send their money to their families to help them survive.

This is fun, I'm enjoying myself, this is kicking the goal. We are in class systems right here on the ship. I am low on the ship. I am one of the lowly. I am on the bottom of the Titanic.

The separation between classes is becoming more evident than before I got on the ship. The people who are taking care of us, serving, and making up our rooms, are just trying to survive. The people on this boat could choose any vacation. But they chose this.

The disparity in our planet is getting bigger and bigger. We do not need to have this kind of glory and magnificence in our life. We need to dumb it down a notch. We don't need all the fucking shit we think we need. We are over the top.

I definitely am getting to know what I like and what I don't like.

I could've easily accomplished what I came to accomplish on a three or four-day cruise. Why a seven-day cruise? I have no idea. But I am assured a seven-day cruise is because I have a lot more to do than I believe I do. I'm going through a transformational place. There's a lot happening. I'm surrounded by people, yet not near anyone. It is magnificent yet annoying at the same time.

I found the spaces where I like to be. Places where I can be in the sun and away from people. I need to be away from people as much as possible. But I'm okay being next to them because I can be isolated. I just don't like them as a rule.

People don't realize it, but when they couple up, they become dependent on another human. Without that other human, they are completely lost if they have to function on their own. I watch these lost lambs looking all around the ship for their other half because, without them, they are not complete. They need each other. They depend on each other. When did this happen? When did we have to depend on someone else to have a meal? To walk the track? You came to fill the void in the other, but you are not to become Siamese twins. I can't wrap my brain around it. Each one of you is so tied to the other you cannot see the forest for the trees. Without them to tell you if it is a forest or an ocean, you have no fucking clue.

I believe most people enjoy cruising because they like the mass amounts of delicious food. There are a lot of very, very obese people here. And I'm sure they are taking total advantage of the plethora of yummies before them. I have a feeling they eat every meal in each of the restaurants every chance they get.

Why do I see seagulls? We are in the middle of the ocean. Did they climb onto the ship?

It feels so delicious to know I could do something like this and be around all of these people with their limited conversations, and they cannot affect me. I can only be affected if I allow myself to engage, and that is virtually impossible. I am not to do small-scale, conversational work any longer. My work is more global. I have much bigger fish to fry. The one on one is no longer.

We have a lot more problems on this planet than individual issues.

This trip is detaching me.

I look at people through a completely different lens now. I look at them as completely lost souls and fucked up beyond comprehension. They do not have a clue how lost they are. I am inventing a new reality, one that has not been introduced yet. My words are going to change the planet. People are going to know me because everything that's been done before is clearly not working.

Every part of me is going to be changed after this experience. I am not going to be somebody connected to television, to anything. I am beginning to see the transformation that I have yet to expect. I will be shedding the layers of family and people that I cannot stand to be around. Because I do not want to be near them. They are energy, sucking, draining and I want nothing to do with them.

We act like we are deserving ones.

To be continued

CHAPTER 35
PUERTO VALLARTA FEARLESSLY

I think this title will be self-explanatory when you're done reading my story. People love to read a good vacation blog. This is one of them.

If you're going to Puerto Vallarta, do the extreme zip-lining adventure with Vallarta Adventures. These guys are the bomb. You do what a normal human would be scared to death to do. The ones who think they want to do it, but know they like to get in their heads, they would die here. Thoughts alone would kill them.

Here, you don't have a chance to weigh your options if you should take a leap or not. There is no time to think. You get suited up, you cross the bridge, and you walk up the hill. By the time you get to the top, you're hooked to your first zip line. There's nobody waiting. You just go. There is no turning back. The vultures are squawking in the trees like wild turkeys. You will stay with your group.

What stunned me about this excursion was how few people came from the ship. When you go to port you have many excursion choices, or you can do nothing at all. My sister recommended this excursion, so I checked it out. Apparently, I found one that was even more extreme than hers. I thought we would have a bus full of young (mostly) adventurers. There were thirteen of us. That was it. I was the only solo adventurer.

These were unique and different zip lines. I've zipped all through Whistler/Blackcomb and it was pretty. It was okay, but my adrenaline wasn't even tempted to be challenged. I did every zip line upside down and still to me; it was just meh. I'm the crazy lady who loves to catapult out of a slingshot. I need a rush.

You are 65 feet up when you step out on the platform wrapped high up on a tree. They clip you in and wave goodbye. Off again, onto another ledge for your first repel. I love repelling. Then, you zip line to the next station. Zip, drop, hike, go. We were all over the map. Any chance I was able, I went upside down. These were all unique. Some you had to hold the cable with your thick leather glove making an "O" shape with your fingers to keep you from flying out of orbit.

The zip-coaster was wild. You're sitting in a diaper with your hands on the sides like a chain on a swing. It is metal and feels like an old-fashioned rickety roller coaster. You feel like your head needs a brace by the time you are done. You fly around a corner and dip down and up. Wild ups, downs, and turns. You're flying through the forest on a zip line. It was a gas. Of course, the photographer captures your best expressive faces.

Back in line 65 feet high up in a tree. On a ledge about 2 feet wide wrapped around the tree. By the time you see what your next adventure is, you are next. They hook you in and you step backward off of the platform in a freefall.

You are hooked in and you know you are safe. You would never even question it. Everybody wants to freefall. You do it in your dreams. Here you get to land gently. You don't have time to think as it is your turn to leap. You just go. More fun zip lines, And then Superman.

They put you on a board and lower you down to strap you in like Superman. Helmet, goggles, and a Go-Pro camera to capture your every expression as your face flattens at 65 miles an hour.

As I was soaring through the trees, I loudly sang Clint Eastwood's, *I Talk to the Trees* from the film, *Paint Your Wagon*. You can see my lips moving in the video but all you hear is the zip of the line.

It was the highlight of all the other highlights. They were all highlights. And then the next highlight was the choice of another zip line or stepping off the ledge. Stepping off the ledge meant a pendulum swing freefall. Who doesn't want to do that? This checked so many boxes. I wanted to go back and do the entire course again so I could take it all in.

After that, there was the most gripping Mexican waterslide, the kind that recommend you continue wearing your helmet. You use a mat like a diaper, lay back, and go. It was a gas. Glad I had my bathing suit on under my clothes.

The only regret was I couldn't climb the 65' net to get to the last high-up adventure. I fell skiing a few weeks prior and landed on my right elbow. It jammed my elbow into my shoulder. I knew I couldn't do this one little thing. In missing it, I missed some of the best parts.

They walked across a tight rope 65' up in the sky with two little ropes to hold onto on each side. Then then walked across a sea of tree tops cut to resemble telephone poles. Just like a tree does in the wind, at 65' up, they were swaying.

Another unexpected gift was something that pushed me beyond something that once was a comfort zone. I was the lady who casually rolled around at the go-kart track. I am not racing anyone. I am just driving as I wish to drive. Here I had to keep up with the lead driver. I was second in line with a four-wheel drive Polaris desert jeep. The roads went all over the place.

At every other time in my life, I would've thought this through. I wouldn't drive the car. I would have deferred to be a passenger. I would've chickened out. I would have talked myself out of it. When I said I was a driver at the start they put that color band on my wrist. I did give myself the caveat that if it was something that bothered my shoulder, I would not do it.

We took turns taking fun pictures with the car before we drove so I knew my shoulder would be fine. I was right behind the pilot car. It was dusty. I had to keep up with him, and I was eating his dust. Behind me was a cloud for everyone else to follow. It was deep sand.

I put the pedal to the metal. I played with keeping my tires deep in the ruts which felt like tracks, or going on top and being higher up. I don't know the rules so I got to play with it. He went fast. I was right behind him. He would stop to wait for everyone to catch up, then off again.

We went around the corner and I stayed close to his tail. There were a few bends where I could easily lose him. We came around the bend and I saw he was in the middle of a rickety bridge over a river. There were big holes in between the center boards. You could not leave the exact center position. Previously I think I may have frozen.

I have a former friend who would've died right there. She would not have survived another moment. I went full speed ahead and drove hard across the bridge. What else could I do? Think about it? I was right behind him. Watching the videos on the Vallarta Adventures website, I saw many drivers going much slower than I did.

I'm so proud of myself that I have no fear. I get to live fully and fully live because this stuff is right there for us all to do. You find reasons not to do things that make you "uncomfortable." The translation for this is fear. Just do it. Get out of your head. You are missing out on so much fun; things that really matter to the soul.

If you just do it, you figure out why you need to. Like when I jumped in without thought to join a group of strangers for an 18-day whitewater rafting trip through the Grand Canyon, down the Colorado River. I bought my provisions in Ohio and met them for the first time at the put-in for our trip on the river. Best 18 days of my life. They all are because I choose to have fabulous adventures. That one was my first highly spiritual experience, and I didn't even know it until years later.

Because of this magical time, I wanted to do it. I wanted to challenge myself to be it. I became a white-water rafting guide on the Wenatchee River in Leavenworth Washington. That town captured my heart. A lovely Bavarian Village with the best camping anywhere, rock climbing areas, too many hikes to list, lakes in the mountains, and lots of white-water rafting. We loved it so much we got married there. We spent many days off in this town. Rock-climbing, white-water rafting, camping, and hiking. It is magical. My child grew up here.

For one season I trained to be a guide. I went through weeks of training in the winter on the cold river. You become a "guide" after you bring a group with you and take them down the river safely. It is your 'guinea pig' test run.

I knew it was something I couldn't do long term, I just wanted to experience it. My mouth was constantly dry because of terror. I was fine when I was with the other trainees and the guides, but when I had children in my raft, I knew I was responsible for their lives. That was too much for me. They are on their journey and I don't want my journey to intersect with damaging theirs. It bothered me back then. I did not know that we did not have control.

CHAPTER 35
MAZATLAN GAVE ME HOPE

This was the best experience ever. Off of the heels of Vallarta Adventures the day before, this was going to be a chill day on the beach, or so I fantasized. Going on a cruise I thought I would be doing all the fun cruise things. My life is not that life anymore. I should have known better. I do not like being on a beach like this. I had to come to Mazatlán. I had to shut up and await my instructions.

We were on a Greyhound-type bus. I was impressed. There were many buses taking passengers all over Mazatlán. It was a pretty solid tour group; a well-oiled machine.

At the front of the bus was the adorable tour guide explaining the town as we went through it. Like they always do, ours said her name which was about eighteen syllables. It always ends up being a name we can't pronounce. The short version for us to call her was Fair Ne. I loved her. Just adorable.

I was in Mazatlán almost 30 years ago with my ex. When the bus pulled into the resort where I would spend the next five hours, it was where we stayed. Out of all of the places I could've ended up, we ended up here. It grew up quite a bit.

When I got to the beach, I remembered I don't want to lay on the beach or sit in the sun. I have never been a fan. I didn't want to do anything. I walked on the beach until our buffet opened.

There was a sign above the bar that said the bartender was making US$16 per hour. This captured me. I wasn't sure what it meant. That seemed interesting as bartenders and waitresses don't make a high hourly rate. Normally, they make their money in tips.

When I saw Fair Ne, I pointed to the sign. I asked her, is this real? She giggled, of course, it's not. I didn't know why they posted it. The motel is now an all-inclusive resort. To me, it didn't make sense, but it started a conversation with this lovely soul.

When I see people, I tell them what I see in them. I love it when I am brought to those with promise. To bright lights. I told her she is a shining star; that she is gifted in what she does. I told her to pursue knowing more and telling more stories. She lit up like a Christmas tree. I don't remember any part of the conversation. I do know I need to keep my recorder going when I speak, but I don't.

She was so excited after our chat, she returned with a group of girls. They were all Sparkle Farkle. Absolutely adorable. All of these girls are the tour guides on the buses. They wear matching yellow shirts and khaki pants. They drop their busloads of people off at the hotel and give instructions on where to be, and when. They make themselves available to their busload for the entire day. These young ladies were the reason I had to go to Mazatlan.

They were all stunning. They were all beautiful. During one of the group conversations when I mentioned the word self-love, they all looked toward Emma; they all pointed to the girl in the middle. The one that clearly lacked self-esteem and self-love.

The words that come through me at a moment like this are brilliant. I am not coming up with things to say to fit the situation, the words that fit the situation flow from my mouth. They are the answer every time.

Emma was reminded that there are no errors, and there is no such thing as normal or a standard we are supposed to live by. We are all exactly what we are supposed to be. She is absolutely perfect. She is exactly who she is supposed to be. On the outside, absolutely stunning. On the inside, questioning everything.

By the time I was done, she was not the same woman. She grew right before all of us. By the time I got back on the bus, I believe there were 15 girls gathered around me. They were a captive audience. They absorbed every word I said. I hugged them all. They all have my card. I told them I am here if they ever need me. People only reach out to me when they need a lift. I would never give anyone a nickel. I can give so much more of my strength through words. And they know it. These girls really touched a spot in my heart.

I was sitting in the shade waiting for nothing when the buses started rolling back in. I saw them jump into action, deploying the crowd, and wrangling the cattle. They were amazing. And they all spoke in their natural style. They were really something to watch in action. We really connected that day. I felt I made a difference in lives that really mattered. I have never had a more captive audience who was so easy to please. I left Mazatlán seeing a changed community.

These girls are going to elevate each other because now they know how. These girls are going to elevate other people because they can. Sometimes you need somebody to lift you up a little bit for a difference to be made.

My website slogan is, "Changing the world by planting one seed at a time." I don't get to see what happens when I leave, I just know so much change happens. That is why I am here.

Newport was my training ground where I worked with one person at a time. Some really big shit unfolded that I was in the middle of. Now, I've been promoted to work with large groups of people.

These girls are amazing and they are going to thrive. They're going to be politicians. They're going to get rid of the bullshit. They are a tribe now. The kind of tribe you want to bump into. They had a few hours with a little unit that showed them they can do or be anything they can dream of. And they can do it without fear. They all grew that day. I look forward to the day when I hear from them again and they update me on their lives. I know they will be rock stars.

My takeaway from Mazatlán was probably the biggest headline for my entire cruise. I don't know what the words would be, but this is what it would be about. Going back to the ship was a bit painful. I was not looking forward to being back with "those people" after witnessing so much potential for the day.

Everyone on the bus, we were waiting for the same couple that kept us waiting before we left. They knew what time to be back. We are all grown-ups here.

Getting on the bus last, they had to go to the back of the bus. In my usual style, I was in the very back row. This woman was short, but she was huge. It took her quite a while to get all the way to the second to the last row. She had to squeeze her body in between the seats. Each time, she gasped for air. By the time she got to her seat, she could barely breathe.

When Fair Ne did the headcount, I knew who was missing. We left shortly thereafter. This tour group runs a tight ship. They have deadlines and we all knew it. Disrespect and lateness annoy me. There is no reason for it. It reminded me of what I was going back to voluntarily.

Not only was this the first time I was on a cruise looking through my new lens, it was the first time I was back in the heart of Mexico. I was spending my time and energy with the people who live there. I was not a visitor. It was magical really diving in and getting to know their stories. I've never done this.

I was leaving a place where everybody is on the same playing field. Everybody sparkles in their own way. Nobody stands out as special. They are all special. They all accept each other exactly as they are. They are the happiest people on the planet. They love. They don't have anything. They are so happy. This is how I like to feel. We are all one.

I've been told in Mexico there are two classes, the rich and the poor. From my eyes, there is the entire population that we all see, then somewhere the rich and powerful are floating around. They do not present themselves in front of us. I truly see a land of equality unlike anything I've seen. They all do something to make a living, and no one is less than anyone else. No one is making it rich in Mexico. They are just living and doing what they need to survive. Their focus is not about making it rich and having "it all." They are good people who come from a space of love.

It is like in The Grinch, in Whoville when he is back on top of his mountain and the village begins to sing. Stuff doesn't matter. They are all together, loving life and each other, and not putting emphasis on "stuff." It is all about love. They don't want to work eighty hours a week at a "career" to make their life into something that it isn't. They want to live by their means and be who they are. This is what we are all here to do. Learn from Mexico.

All you see are the people who work very hard for very little but remain very happy. It's like tribes in native lands that don't know about this reality. It could not be real to them. In Mexico, all they know is what they have. And they are so happy with it.

CHAPTER 36
THE SHIP STORY

I've gone on many cruises, but three as a solo traveler in my adult life. The first one: I left a suicide note in my North Canton, Ohio home. I was going to jump off the ship. Clearly, that didn't happen. The second one: I was there with Hay House; Brian Weiss, Reid Tracy, and Cheryl Richardson. It was a "Speak, Write, Promote" workshop. A very inspirational cruise. I was there for my evolution.

The last cruise I went on was in March. The other cruises I went on with intention. This cruise, I went there believing part of me might have a chance to chill, yet I know better. I knew there was a reason, however, I was the last one let in on it. I thought I might be going to sing and dance the nights away as I cannot do that anywhere near where I live. I knew better. I don't do "vacation."

This has been deep in my soul since I returned from the cruise, but it is time that I share. Knowing it was time, I cried hard in the hot tub. This is an example of why I hate people. What you have become; do you even realize it? I have to pray that you don't. Because if you did, if you saw a movie of you doing what I'm going to describe, I hope you would cry too. I really do.

I was sent on this cruise because I look at life through a new lens now. I am not there to recreate. In Hawaii, people knew it was not a good idea to be out paddle boarding and playing in the sand when people were dying up the road. They asked people to leave the island, and people did. It was heavy. Very heavy.

I understand when you go on a cruise, you plan on eating a lot, drinking a lot, partying by the pool, gambling, enjoying lots of entertainment, playing bingo and games, and doing nothing at all.

Back in the day, going on a cruise you had early or late seating. You had table mates. You knew the same people for the length of the cruise. There is good and bad to both. This cruise was freestyle with many restaurant options. Many, of course, you pay for. The huge dining rooms from the past still exist, with the mass of industrial kitchens. Now people are scattered throughout the ship.

On this ship, for dinner, you had your choice of the big dining room, the massive buffet, Taste and Savor restaurants, a burger joint, or any of the small cafes. Included with your fare were many meal options open to all. With my package, I got one meal at a paid-for restaurant. I chose the steakhouse as they had Bearnaise sauce to go with the steak. Something I enjoy and love to make. It was a wonderful experience. I left a nice tip.

There are so many places to get food or drinks all day long.

Once the elevator hit floor 18, it was like me shopping at Nordstrom's. I didn't want to get out or go any further. The icky feelings are there before the door opens. These floors are where the self-appointed privileged people reside. The people who don't think about how much something costs. They get to mingle with people just like them and compare whatever they think is important at that level. Rich and filthy, you folks are not my jam. They had their own pool, restaurant, and suites. I am glad we didn't have to sit across from each other at dinner. That would have been fun for me, but you would have ended up spending the rest of your trip in your suite hoping to never run into me again.

To get to the go-karts or the laser tag, you had to go by the people of the Ritz as they were on the top of the ship. The energy of people like this is too icky for me. I couldn't go there. I wouldn't want to see the people, let alone feel their stink.

In my other book, I talk a lot about the Power Baby and the Puffy Guy; what people become when they think they are something special. I am not able to be near their energy. It zaps me.

I would choose to be on the bottom of the Titanic when it sailed no matter how much money I had. That is where people speak only the truth. That's who I am. I can't nor would I pretend to be something I am not. How could I? That would be a lie.

At the end of the day, I was definitely not there for a vacation. I met many incredible people. Only the people I was supposed to meet. I helped everyone that I met. The stories are magnificent. They had to meet me. They needed to hear what I had to say. You have no idea what you're missing. There is not one person who leaves my space who doesn't walk away with a message and a glimmer of hope. You get to miss out. You choose to stay stuck in your beliefs.

I cannot believe how hard it is for me to talk about this. I don't carry sadness, but it's a message I know I'm supposed to relay. And I know I'm speaking for thousands upon thousands upon thousands of people. And they need me to speak. Because they can't. If they don't smile, they won't have a job.

4,500 people were there for a vacation. I was there to talk to those who needed me. And I was.

I would like to paint a picture for you.

This is all from my observation. I live alone now in the mountains. Over seven months alone here; a year and a half in Oregon silent before this. I do not talk to people. The only time my TV is on is for me to watch one of the streaming shows that I am guided to watch. There are very few I can tolerate. Human behaviors; I was you. Who I was; disgusts me. The things we do are horrible; we are clueless.

I was fat, and always thought about my weight until 2009. I was constantly arguing with myself and stressing over those pounds. Five, ten, forty pounds overweight. "I must exercise. If I don't, oh shit." I thought about my weight until I got busy doing something that I loved, and I didn't think about it anymore. At that moment, I dropped 20 pounds. And now, I roll around at 110#. Give or take five. I'm in the best shape of my life.

Being on this ship was an eye-opening experience. Being overweight was my choice. I gave it way too much energy. When I decided it wasn't something I needed to think about, food was no longer important, and the weight fell off. Now I eat anything I want, anytime I want. I love good and yummy food. If it's not delicious, I won't eat it. I definitely do not need much. I can't finish an "American" kids' meal. You really should rethink portion size.

We have become gluttonous. You should walk around the buffet area on a cruise ship. Some people require two seats. What a delicious playground for people with very large appetites. I know cruise ship management is happy when they see somebody like me walking on the ship. I won't leave much of a footprint. These people are eating themselves to death. They can, so they will. Many of them need scooters to get around. I know good food is fun to have, but you can have a smaller amount of everything and still be satisfied. It doesn't feel good to be so heavy. I know. I carried extra bowling balls with me as well. My thighs were double in size, maybe even triple.

You do know you chose this, correct? It is not a disease. Neither is alcoholism, but that's another story. Everything is a choice we make. Anything we put in our mouth is on us. If you would like to argue with that, go for it. Anything you say yes to is a choice you make.

You say yes to these buffets, and you must fill up the "Suggestion Box" because they get bigger and bigger to serve more and more needs. With 4,500 passengers, and so many restaurant options, why does the buffet have to be *this* big? Why does it have to be open so often? We have zillions of food choices already. We don't need multiple stations with all of the same things. We can walk around the corner to the station with scrambled eggs, flapjacks, bacon, and waffles. It's so much more than we need.

If the buffet and big dining room aren't enough, pay for the steakhouse, Mexican, French, Italian, or Japanese restaurants. There are options everywhere. The buffet doesn't have to have 5,000 options just so you can scoot your cart around.

I noticed on this cruise they don't do the cute towel folding. It is cute, but I felt unnecessary. Some cruise ships probably have it as a trademark, I don't know. It's just not necessary. I did not miss it. That is the last thing my room steward needed to think about.

I am writing this slowly. I am letting it unfold. I was just shown a vision that sends me back to the story; meaning I need to go back to the heaviness I felt on the cruise once again. That is why I turn it on and off like a switch. I go back to it after I take a breath. But it will all be covered. Believe me. I have to get this out.

I'm also shown that I need to explain the fact that getting something out is important.

If I did not share this ball of darkness that I carried with me from the ship, it would rest inside of me. I get to see what that looks like as a digital matrix. This is what happens to you every time you do something or say yes to something you don't want to do. I don't keep any of this stuff inside. That is why I have to share. I am a vehicle for a reason.

You don't have to share your darkest secrets, but you have to let them go and move on. We all have secrets. That's why we are here. You do not have to repent because we all are humans in a skin bag. We came here to do stupid things. Let it go, move on.

My experience on this cruise ship was beautiful. It was magnificent. I got to know some of the most amazing souls on the planet. I choose not to carry this heaviness like a sponge, so I am sharing, and hopefully, people might look in a mirror and realize they are the problem.

This is why I hate people. I was the only one who went on a cruise to meet people. That is not expected of any of you. But you need to understand the mechanics of making your cruise so spectacular.

On the cruises I've been on before, the entertainment is top-notch. It's why I enjoyed cruising. The piano bar, people singing along with a very talented person. You knew you could catch the performer for a couple of nights. The shows, the entertainers, and many of the crew staff were highly talented entertainers. It was fun. You met people from all over the world working on the ship. They were there happily living their dreams.

This was one of my dreams. I wanted to be a cruise director just like Julie McCoy from The Love Boat. And I wanted to be an entertainer. I did not know they were one and the same until later.

Jobs on a cruise ship are not what they used to be.

After I returned from the cruise, I poked around at working on a Norwegian cruise ship. A position I found required years of training in culinary education and high expectations. In return, you get life on the sea. And your pay rate was $13 an hour. This was a specialized position.

These numbers were told to me by people working on the ship. Out of the 1700 crew, 60% are from the Philippines. I've never been to the Philippines, but it is a place I want to visit. This means on this ship alone; we are floating on the sea with a thousand people who once lived full-time with their people in the Philippines.

After getting to know these people and their situation, I couldn't help but want to see who owns Norwegian Cruise Lines. It looks like it's owned by stockholders. I am sure these stockholders are in some of those suites with the private pool and restaurant. I would not want to meet them. They would not want to meet me. Their lives would never be the same. I can't not speak my truth. I am fearless.

I would like to know how many days a week they work. I would like to know what their living conditions are. I would like to know what their house looks like. I would like to know where their staff is from.

These people I spoke to work seven days a week. I know a lot of you superstars out there work seven days a week. You don't have to. You choose it. You call it workaholism or whatever. Running away from your wife, excuses to stay away from reality. I don't care what you call it. You choose it. These people chose their reality. Here's where I have to stop It gets so hard.

But I won't They can't.

These amazing souls sell their souls to the stockholders, so you can eat all day long at the buffet and get fatter and fatter.

They work seven days a week. They work for four weeks out of the month. They work at least six months out of the year. These amazing souls have to smile because they are replaceable. These amazing souls have families. These amazing souls don't get to see their families. But they do get to sell their soul so you can eat all day long, and not think about their needs. If they thought about their own needs for a moment, it would destroy them. They would all want to die and wish for a sinking ship. If they did that, as a group, they could make their dream come true.

I see this now, but I know it would rip my heart out. I would love to see the living conditions of my room steward. How many are piled in on top of him? How much privacy does he have? Can he at least take a shit by himself? These amazing souls are piled on top of each other at the bottom of your cruise ship. They don't get days off. They don't get to go hang out in Puerto Vallarta. They have to work. They are working because they have a place to sleep. They get to take a shower. And they are fed.

According to human standards, they are being taken care of. However, I can't imagine an American saying yes to their conditions. We say, "We have rights." They say, "We need food." To me, their conditions are not acceptable. Humans have rights and needs. We all do.

These people see it as a benefit. Although they cannot have an existence of their own, they get to send their income home to the Philippines. They get to keep food on the table back home. One lovely soul who works 12+ hours every day, and frequently over time. He does get to talk to his wife and son every night on some Internet line.

I pray to God it didn't cross your mind that he should be fine because he gets to talk to his family. His child doesn't get to see his dad. He is growing up without a father. This man is so full of love. His son needs him in his life for strength and influence.

You couldn't handle it. You could not survive a week of their reality. Barely a day. They have extreme expectations to perform their jobs. And they have to smile. Their insides are dying. But they are doing this because their families need the money. Thousands of people are piled on top of each other on these cruise ships so you can eat more and drink more. I do not see how any of this is okay.

I prayed for a moment when they went home for whatever short amount of time they got, that it was paid time off. I didn't investigate because I knew that was not the case. I pray I am wrong. But I know that would be what an American would demand, or they would not take the job.

I went on this cruise to witness the human condition. The more I saw, the more I grew away from mankind. Man is not kind. Man is evil. You can easily be on the top of the Titanic if you would have nothing to do with those on the bottom. You wouldn't even try to set them free. How can you live with yourself? I can go on and on, but I can't. I have to release this. All I can do is pray for these people.

Well, that's not all Maybe I've started something.

I had great conversations with those that I talked to. I sprinkled my dust and waved my wand. The ones I had conversations with are changed. They are lifted. They can see a future. They see promise. They know there is a way out. And they have friends in their cabin. Sometimes this is the best cancer to catch. One that brings hope. One that inspires. One that gives them a reason for living. Your gluttony certainly does not.

The next time you go on a cruise ship or something to spoil yourself rotten, look in the eyes of the person who's helping you. Dare yourself to ask them what their story is. You don't ask because you don't want to know. If you knew how they were selling their soul to serve you and know that they really cannot stand you, and they despise you and the ground you walk on, perhaps you could look at them in a different light. That guy joking with you behind the bar, the one working every fucking minute of every day. The one that is always there when you show up, he hates you. You are keeping him prisoner.

I remember when cruising was a great job that paid well, and you got to see the world. They worked hard, but they got time to play. Even the room stewards. But your expectations started growing. And now you get lipstick on a pig. The way they provide entertainment is now something I believe was inspired by boy bands.

Rather than paying entertainers what they cost to perform on a ship, providing them accommodations, food, and everything else they need, now they create their own little music stations. They now take the Filipinos who can play an instrument or sing, and create bands. They know they aren't special; it is simply one of their assigned duties on the ship.

They do all your favorite tunes, including the Beatles. He may be Ringo Starr by night, but in the daytime, he's serving you at the Japanese restaurant. Is that really what you want to create? Well, you have. While you are the cat's meow as far as you are concerned, not one thing in their life is special.

Their shift is carrying in all of the equipment and setting it up. They do their music set for three hours, then they tear down their equipment and put on the uniform for their next assignment that day.

You keep perpetuating their horror. How can you live with yourself? Why do you think I can't look at you guys? Why do you think I can't be around you people? This is okay with you? This is not okay with me. This actually puts a divide between me and you like you cannot imagine. People like you have storage units to keep all of the shit you can't get rid of. We cannot be friends.

And no I don't give a rip about you or what you're doing. I am a channel. I am someone who is sent to look at what is going on and to report back. My eyes are the ones used and I have a panel going through me at all times who uses me as their vessel. When it sounds angry, somebody is. I could give a rip. But somebody has to point this out because clearly, privileged folks can't see it. Why would they? It would change their reality. They like living in "style." You keep perpetuating this bullshit by saying style is important. You all make me sick.

What you can't understand about people like me is when you hear us talk, you are inspired. You find a glimmer of hope somewhere inside. It doesn't take much. The way our lives are going, the way this planet is going. For those of us living in the United States, we are the most powerful country on earth, right? Isn't that what we thought? Isn't that how we were raised? And now you are literally believing you have no choice but to choose icky or ickier as your great leader. And you trust that this is your only option.

Would you have stayed in line and walked in the showers? You might want to think about this. I say you did without question.

CHAPTER 37
WE'VE BECOME INSIGNIFICANT

I did not go there to party, sing, dance, and drink the night away. I went there to meet the people who work on the ship, the ones serving you on the ship. I met the people who desperately miss their families. I met people who don't know what it is like to not work and live Groundhog Day. I met some magnificent people, and they can't speak for themselves. I saw the condition of their life. I saw the pain in their hearts. I promised them I would do something about it.

You have luxury and space in the penthouse on a cruise ship while they are piled on top of each other on the bottom. This is not okay with me. You paying a fortune for a cruise vacation with "tips included" should trickle down from the cruise penthouse to the servants piled on top of each other. But no, they don't see the money. Most of them never see a tip. They barely see anything.

Where do they find enough people to fill these jobs? We have a generation of couch potato, coddled kids who won't work the low-paying jobs on the ship. They are paid to stay at home.

You must have your restaurant options, so they bring in servants to meet your needs.

Rich people, stockholders, and board members live in mansions. Why did we allow money and power to become your leader? The people with the most power and money can get away with anything. And they do. You are saying you are okay with it. I am not okay with it. I'm not and that's why I'm writing this book. If you don't realize what you're allowing, there is something wrong with you.

These people are working for the rest of their lives on the ship, their families are getting by. They will not be together. They are disposable humans apparently. Their lives don't matter. The only lives that matter are those with power and money. That is what America has been saying for far too long. If you don't have power or money, you do not matter. You are disposable.

You want to take care of the elegant and significant humans who adorn themselves in lovely jewels and designer labels. They are what matters. That is why we watch them on television and we want to be like them. They are important and we are not. We want to wear clothes like them, to look like them, because we are insignificant.

I hope you realize that is the message you are sending to the planet. What matters to you is the rich, powerful, and those with. America has shown that that is what we need to be in order to live on this planet. The dreams, the goals; they are about money and power. What we can be when we grow up is based on dollar signs. We are the sickest country on the planet.

When I went to Canada 30 years ago to go skiing, I saw the Canadian music video channel. If it's a Canadian artist, they have a Maple leaf. And then an American artist came up, nothing. They have many artists in Canada and nobody knows who they are. They just do what they like to do for a living. They play guitar and sing. They make videos. Same with actors.

People don't strive to sing and become actors because they will be rich and famous in Canada. It is just another job. The same with Europe. Taylor Swift was with a very significant man in that country as far as our standards are concerned. Who knew who he was? The only thing we know about Europe is the royal family.

In our country, we put people who can carry a tune and say lines on a page in front and above. We have put people who happen to be born into a famous family on TV and suddenly they are who everybody wants to be like. Everybody emulates these people who are rich and famous; making them richer and more famous. Remember when the Cosby family was the family to be like? Now look at the debacle. How about Aunt Becky?

Why are we about lifestyles and society? We are looking at people on television and on magazine covers and videos, and we are trying to mold ourselves into something that is not us. We are none of this. We need to stop this insanity. The people who should make the most money in our country are the people who help other people. People who can sing, dance, and act should be paid no more than teachers, painters, or social workers. Your priorities have created our payment structure.

Your social media has given you standards that you think are the standard you need to live by. If I were you, I would throw your phone in the toilet and never look back. Get out of your house. Who you have become is toxic. Screens kill us. We kill ourselves because of expectations and we will never live up to them.

There are no expectations. You are creating this. There is nothing we are supposed to be or do when we are here. We are supposed to shut up and allow our story to unfold. When you're trying to squeeze yourself into a tube of toothpaste, and you know you will never fit, you will die trying. I am saying stop it. I am giving you permission.

You are not who you are trying to be. You don't know who you are because you've never met yourself. You met you when you were little. You loved that part of you. That was the part of you that you wanted to express and be for the rest of your life. You knew this was your sparkle suit if you allowed yourself to step into it. But then when they picked you up and flung you across the room, and told you how lowly your life would be, you started losing the glimmer of hope that shined bright days before. Over time, you realize anything you dreamed of as your future reality was being overshadowed by the reality that life is not going to be pretty. We come here with a plan, and we are very aware that we may never find our first breadcrumb to get us on our path.

If we allowed our children to step out of the crib and into their lives, and let them become who they are, they would be magical miracle workers from the get-go. They will be the changemakers. They will show the world that when you're allowed to step into who you planned on becoming, you are suddenly a useful and productive member of society. You know your role and you are able to step into it quickly and naturally. We need more people without a leg up to step into their roles. Those with a leg up are screwed from the get-go, but if they are willing to listen to the only voice that matters, they can find their way here. That leg-up thing is a really bad idea.

If you sit and think about the logic behind this, you know, it makes sense. You remember your childhood and your dreams. We all do. And then we remembered when they were squashed. But they were still our dreams. Neale donald walsh's, *conversations with god* spells it out magically. We are to come to this planet and become who we are. Find our path. When we step into our path that we planned, the partner and the miracles for that path will unfold.

The way we do it is so wrong. We want to model the parents who met and fell in lov, ot married, and locked into a life that they swear they are going to stay in until they die. We truly are not meant to be married or together forever. We meet people along the way, and we give each other a gift, then we are to move on.

As humans, we created marriage. We need to uncreate everything. Have your partner as long as they are to be there, and then let go. Do not let money and comfort be a thing that keeps you there because then you do not leave. We all need to be equal. We all need to trade what our gift is and share. If you have apple trees, and I have plum trees, we will exchange. If you're good at making shoes and I can make bread, we can share. We all have talents to make everything we would ever need. We are a society that could share if we just allowed ourselves to evolve into our natural talent.

But we have created a reality that is not real. One that you considered to be important. One that is killing us once again. We are destroying our planet. I see ash and rubble. We can only go so high, and we can only get so mad. Those of you who are angry over the election; many of you, your hearts will just burst right out of your chest. One way or another, we will kill each other, we will die of anger.

My way is just letting it all go and allowing your natural course to unfold. Don't stick your head in what's going on just because you have a phone and you can. That is what is killing you. Imagine how peaceful you would be if you didn't know everything you know. But you choose to want to know it and so you are also committing suicide.

We need to get rid of all machines. We need to go back to the human being who has the best plan and the best idea standing before us. We want to see the person before us that we can trust in what they say, believe what they mean, and know they will follow through on it. We need to hear their ideas. The country needs to vote for the one they like the best. The one that represents them and their family and their beliefs. Not take a chance on one and see how it turns out. How has this worked out for us so far?

People aren't voting because they don't know what the hell to do. It's confusing and you've made it confusing on purpose. The harder the language to understand, the more it will be avoided.

That is just like spirituality. People throw so many words out there that even I cannot comprehend. That's why I wrote the books that I wrote. I want to dumb it down to what is real. Simple terms, simple reality, not fancy it up with terms that are so out of this world people don't get near it.

We have gone away from what we came here to do. We are not even close. We are completely destroying our planet. We need to topple the towers; they need to be back to ground level. I believe toppling towers is necessary. Especially, the ivory ones. The more delusional we are about money and power, and seeing it as the way, the further away from reality we get. We are so far away from our way home. In order to erase the layers you have created between you and God, you've got to get out of your tower. You have got to get out of that glass castle before it crumbles.

This is urgent. After this election is over, half of you are going to go insane. What happens when your boy is not behind the podium? You are going to go stark-raving mad. You're going to do anything you can to get this back on track. The way your boy said it had to happen.

We are sickening. We have become something so disgusting we can't even recognize ourselves. Do you enjoy living in anger? Can you not sleep at night because your blood is boiling? Do you enjoy this? Your body is not made for this. It will have a short lifespan. I am grateful. We need to thin the herd. Self-inflicted suicide comes in handy. You are choosing your anger. You are choosing to pick a pony and let that pony be the thing that decides how the rest of your life unfolds. You have given your power away.

CHAPTER 38
JOURNALING CONTINUED – NEW LENS

Most of these people are from the Philippines. They work six or seven months and then they are off for a few. They work every single day when they are here. They all have multiple jobs. They don't get to go into port because they are usually scheduled to work on one of their jobs on the ship. They send their money home to their family so they can survive. There are 1700 people working on this ship. The cruise director is from the Philippines. The assistant is a woman from the United States. I would love to see their employment contracts. Americans have standards. The people working on this ship (and others) are desperate.

When did we become so glutenous that we had to grab a net and fill the bottom of the boat with low-wage servants? How about lowering our expectations since an entire generation won't work.

I have a great idea, let's not expect as much when we travel. Let us settle for simple so these humans can be that once again. You do know they are human, right? They are living on the bottom of a ship for months on end without seeing family. They have feelings. I guarantee many tears are shed on the bottom of this ship at night.

I used to cruise a lot. And now it's different. Rich, disgustingly fat people are all over this boat.

Fat and disgusting humans with way too much money, way too much means, and no compassion for anybody. These working people have to smile every single day and say good morning. If they don't, they will be replaced. They do this because they have no choice. It's the only way for them to survive. They are making no money. What they do make, they send home to keep their families alive. Even the performers.

This is where I really saw the difference. They used to have actual performers from all over the world. Now they are people from the Philippines who can sound like the Beatles, who can sound like Kansas, who can sound like anybody. My heart is broken for these people. They are a band by night and a waiter in the afternoon. They are never allowed to feel special. It is their job.

In Mazatlán, I sat down with the tour guides. I handed 15 business cards out, and I sat in a circle with them. They are gaining power as we speak. They are no longer going to be small. I'm creating an army all over the world. I am not looking back, just dictating.

There is a guy at the hotel, Playa Mazatlán, whose job it is to displace the water around the pool. To even it out. He gets a mop, and he evenly mops it so it dries quickly. Then goes to another space and does the same. Then goes right back to the formerly dry spot as it is wet again. Rinse repeat. Rinse repeat. Rinse repeat. Are you fucking kidding me? Have we grown so anal that we need to have the water removed from the pool area? I don't know what's happened to us. It is not good.

I can't wait to get home. I feel like everything I had to do I've done. I saw everything I needed to see. I don't want to put these people through any more hell and turmoil than they've already gone through. I feel horrible for their lifestyle. But for Americans, we whitewash it. We act like it's not happening right before our eyes. They have these guys that have to sound like the Beatles. Yet they have a song called *Eight Days a Week*. That is what these people work. They work eight days a week. They send their money home. I am going to be on a rampage.

Can someone help me understand how this is okay and acceptable? How can all of these fucking fat white people agree that we can make slaves out of the souls from the Philippines? We can sit here and be gluttonous, prim and proper, and have more money than God, and we expect them to wait on us, and please us.

More than anything, I realize I do not like people. There is nobody like me out here anywhere. Not even close. All of these people here have expectations of how they deserve to be treated at their status level. Who in the fuck decided that we have status levels? They did. They feel more special than the people on the bottom of the Titanic. I am so done with people.

I gave up my reservation at the steakhouse for a couple last night as they showed up a day early. I fly solo, I can easily flow. They were thrilled. I ran into them later that night after their delicious steakhouse dinner. They were so happy. I would do it again. Why are people so horrible? Why are they so selfish?

I realize I really do fundamentally hate human beings. I do not wish to be around anyone of these fucking specimens that I'm sitting next to in this classy steakhouse on the cruise ship. Some of these jackasses are buying dinner for 20 or 30 people. Isn't it fun when you can show people how rich you are? I hate people. I don't know what my message is, but this is not it.

People get pregnant, and they think yeah, let's do this thing. Let's be parents. And then suddenly, their life is completely ruined. Why do we do the things we do? I don't know how much longer I can do this.

Cruises can cost the same amount of money, but we need to lower the expectations of the human being. We need to not make it assumed that every fucking whim and desire will be met. There will be limitations. There will be breakfast time, lunchtime, and dinner time. Let's be real. Let's not kill these people for our pleasure. Let's have more fun doing other things, and less time eating.

Have you looked in a mirror naked or stepped on a scale lately? I carried 20-40 extra pounds my entire life. Finally, I am tiny and fluid. I love being small. We don't need food the way we believe we do. When you come from a space of love and light, you will realize you filled a big empty space by pushing things in your mouth. Now I forget to eat.

Before I left my elegant steakhouse dinner, I felt bad that I couldn't do more for these people. Then they gave me a tip receipt. All of the other restaurants, everything is included. These people went beyond the call of duty for me. I was happy to have the chance to personally give them a big tip.

Friday – Cabo. I didn't go to shore today. I knew I did not want to. I was looking forward to an empty vessel. Then came the announcement from the captain. He explained to people waiting to leave the ship that the tenders were slow because of the unrest in Cabo. There was a protest going on. The protest doesn't affect the paid shore excursions, but they are stopping the people who are walking freely off of the ship. That would have been me. I didn't have a plan for Cabo.

It is hitting me at this moment that once I go home, I will not recognize the life I left behind. I have been very peaceful here. Surrounded by zillions, but completely alone and isolated. My reality is going to change drastically. I shall feel nothing and allow.

The magnitude of what I have written is coming through. I can't let it sink in. Nothing can ever sink in. It has to be what it is. I can't allow emotion to step in. I need to move beyond this. The magnitude of my life is unexplainable. No one can possibly comprehend it. I can't.

My family would be the only people I could share these feelings with, but they can't be there for me. I'm not allowed to be myself with them. That has been made abundantly clear. They have lost me.

Most of me feel like I've done everything I came here to do. But of course, the rest of me knows that's not the case. Who knows what's about to happen? I do know people are going to be whining and crying and telling people about their horrible stories. The poor babies had to move faster than they would normally want to move. They had to get back to the ship. The port closed because of the demonstration. They had urgency because they were scared. When you're scared, it's amazing you can lift up a car. People are so fucked up. I want to be further and further away from humans than ever.

We have to get out of Cabo because there is unrest. People are going to be whiny and complaining that their little walking excursion into Cabo ended too early. Wow. Do you really want to be there when there is unrest? Getting back on the ship is really a smart idea. Do the \ math.

Not soon enough – home tomorrow. Today is cool and cloudy. People will be pissed. Not me. Heaven.

Everything I thought I was coming here to do; I did not do. I did not dance. I did not sing karaoke. I did not stay up late. I did not party like a rock star. I stayed away from people. The people I was supposed to be brought to, I met. I love watching how people stare at me when they listen. They want more and more and more. They just can't get enough.

I am different. I am sitting in the dinner hall, the big room that used to be the group dinners. I came here for my last dinner on the ship. The main restaurants all have the same food. You just pick the time and ambiance you are looking for.

I do not like this at all. I absolutely hate it. I will never cruise again. I thought I was going to be doing my seminars on cruise ships. Not under these conditions. Maybe I should start my own fleet. Let these kids be the ones who run and profit from it. Start fucking the Americans.

The world is changing. They are re-introducing slavery in what you must think is an acceptable formula. It's hidden behind your gluttonous pleasures. You fucking humans that require endless food choices and want them to kiss your ass and express your anal glands. Yet you can't even bother to put on a decent shirt for dinner.

I am beyond accommodating to my waiters. When they give me an option, I say yes. I don't want to give them any flack whatsoever. Unfortunately, too many people do. They can't feel what I do.

Monday was a very heavy day. I felt the weight of the people as I left the ship. I felt that I was their hope. Will I say the right thing? Will I do the right thing?

I live my life by following guidance. I was guided to Mexico, I was guided to the ship, and I was guided to those adorable tour guide girls. I hope some of the words I said stick with them. They are beautiful souls. They have so much potential.

I feel in Mexico it is an equal playing ground for everybody. There is nobody who rises above and shines, looks better and cleaner, and has more than everybody else. Not from the lens I look through anyway. They have more of an equality about them. As opposed to the white man in America and the ship. Equality is the last thing anybody wants. They want to be the one with the most. I hate people. I do not like being in America. We are disgusting.

Knowing that Larry the bartender lives Groundhog Day for seven months. He wakes up every day and does the same routine. The only thing that changes are the faces. They are new every Sunday.

He lives Groundhog Day. He is not complaining. And here I am whining. I have this big house, this land, this much potential. Now what? I stand still and say, "Now what?" And I await guidance.

What am I not hearing?

I await guidance. When I go and I do, I get redirected to where I'm supposed to be. I know better. Not one part of my day-to-day, do I do on my own. Now I feel like I'm in wait mode. How do I help? I know standing before those girls, I made a difference. I can't help them from my house. I don't know what to do. I know I will be guided. In the interim, I will do nothing as usual.

I want to go home.

This life has been a miracle. This life has been a gift. I have reached the end. I have done all I needed to do. And now I sit alone in this big house with my birds, my chipmunks, and squirrels, my crows, and I stay still, waiting.

CHAPTER 39
WHY I WENT TO MAUI

The example that I hope to God will open your eyes. It is Friday, March 29, 2024. My life is always magical. Constant miracles unfolding. When you don't live from your human self, you know how to live in a world of magic. It just is. And it is fun. There is a lot of heaviness that goes with it because we are here for a reason. It's not all rainbows and butterflies. Somebody has to do the hard work. Somebody has got to face the hard stuff and report back.

At 5 o'clock this morning, I woke up crying and shaking. I just received an instant download telling me the rest of the story I need to report about. It was so clear that it hit me like a truck. I received downloads like this before. You're suddenly in the scene experiencing everything everyone experiences all at once. It can be horrific. But you understand why you need to deliver the message quickly. It is painful. It is dirty and it is ugly.

It's really hard as a human being to translate what is coming through – thinking we could possibly be this stupid. I don't think we can be this blind as to allow this to happen. It is happening right before your eyes, and you don't see it.

We have had major stories in history of people in power doing really crazy things. You all get mad and wave your fingers at those people because they are wrong. I believe some of you are so busy looking at where you want to point your finger, that you don't even realize you are where you are pointing. You've been on the roller coaster following them relentlessly without realizing it. You are saying, "Do as I say; not as I do." You need to look at your behavior. You need to look at your moral compass. You need to see where you come from.

People wonder why I say I hate people. Because I'm looking at them from the outside. I can see them in a way that I am praying they can't see themselves. I am praying that just the evolution of stupidity has been the natural flow for them, that they haven't looked in a mirror long enough to see what they are doing. I'm not talking about what they're doing for themselves. I'm talking about what they are doing to others along the way. We are stepping on people and not even realizing it. I am hanging tight to the premise that you don't realize it. Because if you have any idea what you are doing, I don't want to be human anymore. We have crossed a line.

As a world, we have become something horrible. And everybody keeps saying yes to it.

While my other book is going to explain everything, and it can change lives, it is not the book I came here to write. It explains me. The book I came here to write is this one. Seven months ago, I was sent to Maui. Now I know why. It was not just for the island and the people at the time. I have a much bigger story coming out of it.

I was shown why I was brought to Maui.

I was brought to Maui where people are paddle boarding, parasailing, swimming, and having a blast. Then it caught on fire. People were asked to leave the island. Doing the humane thing, people packed up and headed to the airport. Humans did the right thing by respecting the island and the people enough to know it's not wise to have a great vacation as people are suffering right up the road. That's humanity. That's just the right thing to do.

Then I go on a cruise where everybody's partying and having a good time. I was there with a whole lot of you. Did you not see what I saw?

Seven months ago, I went to Hawaii, and the island caught on fire. You were asked to leave the island, and you did. You packed up your family, your room, or your timeshare, and you flew back home. It hurt no doubt, but you knew it was the right thing to do.

How can you be on a cruise ship eating, drinking, frolicking, and having fun? You know just a few floors below you people are stacked on top of each other every single day of their existence. They don't see loved ones or get hugs from their kids. They are on this vessel spending their lives on the sea so that you can eat more than any human should consume.

In Maui, you all saw what was happening. It was hard and the kids weren't happy, but you left the island. Now you are on a cruise ship with over a thousand human beings from one little island piled on top of each other, living Groundhog Day because you believe you deserve to be served in a certain way. You demand more so they have to deliver more.

Leaving the island was doing the right thing. Sailing while people below are suffering is not okay. I don't know how you can live with yourselves.

Part of a text message sent to my ex after the download:

The panel that comes through me is what is doing the writing. Alden is on the panel; I found out last night my grandfather joined the panel. This is why I'm using his words as the title.

You live in the land of privileged. You believe kids need to start out with money and a foot up above everybody else. That immediately fucks up their journey. They immediately can't know their path because they have one chosen for them, and they are so confused. This is why people kill themselves. It's all going to be in the book I've got to get to writing.

Things that I've done over the last eight months haven't made a lot of sense, but they never do. I always follow that one step. Taking it, it eventually shows you why you took it. I was sent to Hawaii two days before the island burned. Now I know what my message has to be for this planet.

Thank you, Grandpa, for planting the seed. You were a wise man. I grew up in a place that did not feel like it represented what you were saying. I wondered, "How is man ruining his nest?"

He was a wise man. A great prognosticator. Apparently, nobody listened to him. You are probably not going to listen to me either. But I hope if anything, this story will help you check your moral compass. You need to find where you stand on all of this. You need to sit with yourself and ask, is this really what you stand for?

CHAPTER 40
CRUISE AFTERBURN

How do you feel about terrorists? Satan or the devil? What energy do you spin toward Hitler? What do you think of the drunk driver that took down your family? What about that candidate in the U.S. race that you ***do not*** want for president? What word would you use to describe what you feel about these experiences?

Let me explain to you what I mean when I use the word hate. First, I will explain what I mean when I use the word God. Growing up, I had no religion. We weren't exposed to anything that would explain what people who go to church know and believe. We were completely clueless. I am so grateful for this as I found my breadcrumb trail seven years ago. That trail led me down the path of spirituality.

When you are floating down this river, you discover things that are unexplainable. You realize human language is beyond limited. There are no words to describe experiences that people have who deal with the other side of the veil. We don't need language over there. Consciousness is all we need. Here we have to put a label on it for you to judge it one way or the other.

When I first started this journey, I referred to that thing outside of myself that was so much bigger as higher power, source, source energy, the universe. I had no label for anything. There were no words for things that I experienced. As I found my breadcrumbs and I started turning over every leaf, climbing every tree, and looking under every rock, language is a huge problem on our planet. If I say something that triggers a word that is off to you, like hate, God, or terrorism, it triggers something in you.

When we don't attach labels to things, nothing can be triggered. In much of the work I do, people don't want to move further on because I've triggered something deep within them. It is out of my control. The triggers are the things you need to address. These are the things you must turn and face as they are your line in the sand.

Trying to squeeze a God-reality into human language is virtually impossible. I went through my transformation from the third to the fourth dimension, then catapulted into the fifth dimension. When I realized I was experiencing life at a level beyond human comprehension, the only word I could resurrect out of my knowledge base that could be used to describe the place where I was landing, was the thing you call God.

It was the only thing so much bigger than me, beyond my comprehension, that if I had to put a label on it, it had to be something beyond my comprehension. For my vocabulary, I chose and have been using the word God as the thing that is above all things. Knowing that we are all equal, and we are all sparks of the same star. We are all consciousness. All of us together as one massive creation, we are God. We collectively are God. Our thoughts create how this planet goes. That's what this dictation is about.

Being in the fifth dimension, I do not experience emotions. I live in the land of enlightenment. Here, my emotional state is ineffable, and my view of life is, that it just 'is.' I am that I am. I am heaven, still in a body, but I am in a skin bag that does not function as yours does. Mine is immaculate. Mine is without illness or disease. Mine is no longer used as an earthling in pain with problems. I can't have them. I am unflappable. Nothing matters to me. I know none of this is real.

My isolation has been for a reason. When you are not exposed to human energy, people that hear what everybody else is saying, people that get angry, people that have issues; I don't hear any of this. I live in the land of silence, bliss, and peace. I don't get involved in the stuff that is driving you all crazy. I cannot. If I did, I would not be able to do the work I do. That is what separates those of us who listen to our higher selves from those of you who listen to the news and your neighbor.

What I have witnessed in human behavior over the last years, and in seven days on a cruise, the only word I can describe that I will explain in this manifesto is hate. People who do horrible things, and affect other human lives or animals, I cannot love them. I can't even like them. They are not in my universe. They are here to do horrible and tragic themes. That is their story. I have no problem with that.

I on the other hand cannot be associated with them or near them. Because it would affect my energy. My energy is what has brought me to the line of ineffable. If I sunk deep into the human story, let you whine about the conditions, let you complain that your beautiful dress won't be here on time for the prom. I cannot join you in this. The things that matter to you do not matter to me.

It is with all love and respect for mankind that I say, yes, the only word that can describe how I feel about those of you who treat others like they do not matter. That word is hate. I don't feel the emotion of hate. I remember that. Hate was just a twist on love. Hate was desperation. I am not desperate.

I work with a panel and together we are here to open the eyes of those of you who perhaps forgot how to see. When you see what you all as a collective are doing, it is my prayer and hope that you will do something about this.

We have gone so far left of center that we forgot why we are here.

Language is just something to paint a picture. God is that thing greater than us that is unexplainable. Hate is the collective agreement that humans who are not treated properly, the perpetrators need to be dealt with. When you read the story, you are going to see you are the perpetrator. You are the one doing this. Because of you, people are suffering. I hope to God this is a wake-up call. If it isn't, I don't know if this world can bounce back.

Those in America used to know the land of the free, and we were the powerful nation. I know that is no longer the view, it could not be. We've gone downright stupid. The things we put forward as our priorities, common folk cannot wrap our brains around it.

As far as what you know as hate, as a word, I cannot feel that feeling. All I do is love. That is all we truly are is love. But when the collective decides to become something, and they pretend like they don't realize what they are, that is where I have a problem. That is what I am here to point out.

I was sent to Hawaii two days before the fires to be there for the people. I was sent on this trip to be there for the people. Not the people who are cruising and eating more than any human needs to consume in seven days, but the people who are being kept. The people who are not free. These are the people I love. They are the ones I am here to help.

Remember, I represent no one but my own little self with everything I say. I am never around humans. Everything is my take on anything I see. I am not influenced by you. You cannot influence me. If you do not like what you are reading, delete it. Throw it away. Getting mad at me is stupid. It is one woman's opinion. Don't give me so much power. Move on. Hopefully, I can save one life. It doesn't have to be yours.

CHAPTER 41
LAYING THE FOUNDATION

Before this book came to be, I had a vision of myself on a path where I was laying bricks through a field making a road. I am far away, and the path is long. And I'm laying one stone at a time that seems to appear before me as I place them.

You are all still standing at that gate. It's a long fence, but a wide-open gate. One person is finally willing to be the first to put their toe over the line. They all want to. They want to say yes, she's right. But agree with me, and they go against everything that they've been taught.

Who wants to be known as the brave soul, who is the first one to cross that line? There are so many people on this planet who are stuck with a line in the sand that they cannot get beyond. They want somebody to tell them that it's okay to stay stuck.

We have no leaders anymore. We felt leadership before. And now we are flailing because we don't have any leaders. And I'm here to tell you that you are the leader. You are the one we've been waiting for. You are the strong one. You are the one stuck in a suit that you do not want to wear. I don't care if that's a business suit, a fat suit, a racist suit, whatever suit you are wearing take it off and walk through that gate. Be the first. I did it. So, you're not the first.

The simple truth is you planned your life. You planned the stories that you are involved in. Everybody you have bumped into in your life. We're all part of the plan. I'm not explaining spirituality to you in this book. But you can have access to it in my other books. You chose this life. You also chose to be born into the family you were born into. The goal for every single person who is born is to be who they are. To follow their own very personal arrow. The journey that they created before they were born.

Being born into these situations that seem virtually impossible to walk out of tells me you are an advanced soul. You are somebody that is ready for the hard stuff. The easy way is to stay there and do what everybody tells you. The hard way is saying 'This doesn't feel good and I'm leaving.' The truth is, we came here with nothing, and we truly are happier when we have nothing. But when you have so much, it's almost impossible for you to fathom how life could even be imaginable when you have nothing.

It's literally the flip of a switch. If you make the decision to say yes to you, and to let whatever your natural plan was unfold, you will be the happiest person on the planet, next to me. Once you say yes to you, you find a way to love yourself. Once you love yourself, you find gratitude in the things that make you happy.

The things that make you happy are not shiny and don't cost a thing. The things that make you ultimately the happiest you can ever be are waiting for you after you say yes to you. You did not come here to be a programmed robot. But you are. You are doing what you were programmed to do. It's time to pull out that power pack and replace it with your own energy. Start driving your own bus. Don't let anybody have domain over you ever again.

Once you find the path to yourself, once you get in your lane, you will never let anybody budge you out of it ever again. You will see what feeling good all the time feels like. You will never let them bump you out of your lane again.

In closing this passion project that came through me in less than two weeks, what I want to emphasize is the truth. If this world started to shake and tumble, and cracks started to open with people falling in, those of you at the top of the towers – you become as insignificant as pond scum. Your money cannot buy your way out of the apocalypse.

What I guarantee you would do; you would try to buy somebody like me to show you the way out. And you know what somebody like me would do, I would lead the way because there are others who deserve to know how to get out. Follow if you like. But at least know where you stand. Know your place in line. You may have everything as far as the standards we have created on this planet. But in the end, you have nothing. Without what we carry, you do not exist. You are worthless. You're not worth the paper you are printed on.

If we knew something was coming and the world was in trouble, could you feel comfort turning on the television for answers knowing Walter Cronkite, David Brinkley and Peter Jennings are no longer around? Where would you turn to access feelings of comfort or safety? Who would you trust to help you keep your children safe?

I promise when this world begins to rumble and we know the end is near, you will not see people like me hiding or running away. We will lead you to the safest space on the highest mountain. We will shine our light to show you the way. We know better. We are fearless. We know whatever is coming is a result of how you've been thinking for centuries.

For this world to start on a good course, we need to get back on equal footing. We have gone down the wrong path. No one is special. No one is significant. You may be physically stronger, but that's it. You have nothing on me.

I say the things many of you are thinking but are scared to say. You're scared to even like my stuff on Facebook. If you do, even though you follow me relentlessly, you know people will see that you have responded and that is not okay. You are to stay back with the small people. Let significant and powerful people pound their chest and keep you small.

I am telling you – you are not. Every single one of us has equal footing, you just dress differently. And you've said yes to it. We have so much power. We are unlimited. We are spirits in a skin bag here to learn a lesson. I believe the lesson you have to learn is right before you. Are you going to do the right thing or what is easy? Don't think about it. What feels right? When you change your thoughts, it's like flipping a switch and stepping into a new reality. Change your thoughts, you will change your reality instantly. It is law.

With these words, I am speaking my truth. It is not aimed at anyone. It is aimed at us for allowing it to happen. I must remind you that your reality is out of control. It is so far beyond appropriate and you don't even see it. You've been pregnant with this life for so long, it feels okay. It seems right and normal.

You are living in the land of Oz. You need to get back to basics for a hot minute. You need to remember why you are here. You are not here to be somebody's robot. This is what you have become.

No one is to blame for anything. We choose our path. Even if we find ourselves in a family that does not fit with us. If we stay, that is on us. If we stay, we will manifest all kinds of disease, and a reality that does not feel good inside.

Deep down inside, you know what feels good. You know where you want to be. But the bridge between where you are and where you want to be is too far to cross. Crossing the bridge exposes you. Everyone can see you cross. You know it's like defecting from the Amish, it is a one-way bridge.

You have permission to cross that bridge. Everyone on the planet has permission to cross that bridge. It is the bridge between the reality that you naturally flowed into, and the one that you want. It is your birthright. It is your duty and the reason you were born.

Once you access that space and you become who you were born to be, you can check the box. You learned the lesson you came here to learn. You will not repeat this lesson ever again.

Always remember those feelings when you do not feel good. You will have those in every lifetime, and you can always change your reality. Your record is skipping. Your needle is not in your groove. Once your needle stops skipping and finds its groove, it is smooth sailing. You don't have to do the work. You just have to decide that you are more important than this reality you are pretending to live in. You are part of a play. You have the current page of the script and you know what to say. You no longer have to be this. You can step out of it, step into your reality, and see where it takes you. Learn how to live this way in this lifetime. It will be quickly developed next time around.

CHAPTER 42
PURPLE PEOPLE EPILOGUE

Going back to our story about the young poor purple couple who traded babies in the hospital and took home royal blood. What do you think became of them? The answers are simple.

We have an internal compass when we are born. When we are allowed to let it unfold, to become what it is, it follows its course quickly and naturally. It can't not happen. When you are not told what you cannot do, you can do anything. If you were born in the woods and were raised by a pack of wolves, what do you believe your limitations would be? You would be as limited as the wolves you run with. You would know you could do what they do. That would be it.

The baby who grew up poor will be able to become who they are supposed to be quickly and without any wavering whatsoever. They are on a direct course with their reality from the moment they entered their skin bag. Being without and poor, not having anything, they don't have anything to worship or cling to. All they have is their arrow and they follow it relentlessly. When you are placed on your path, you find your way.

Their child was put through preschool that was registered for before they even made a baby. Every royal child is to go through this education system; including boarding schools, etiquette training, and of course the proper universities. Only the best. If they were not smart enough to get into the proper universities by test scores or athletic abilities, the king and queen would be able to offer an abundant exchange. You make our kid look smart, and your house will never be taxed again.

Their line-up of offspring must know how to walk, talk, be clean, and be poised to appear as a royal should appear. It is merely training. It is programming. It is all we can possibly know when that is how we have been trained. Even before we caught our first breath, we knew what story we were stepping into.

The chances of the stupid baby in the royal clothing ever figuring out what their path is are slim to none. When you have layers and layers of programming on top of you, and you have every possible form of security surrounding you; you know the threat if you even think about defecting from the family. You would be on your own, and you know you would never survive. You will never leave.

The ones who step out of the reality that was not of their creation are the strong ones. They are the ones who survive. They end up discovering who they were when they came here. They can make sense of the thoughts they had and the things they wanted to touch, feel, and do. The burning fire churning in their belly is finally being heard. They were not allowed to be or do any of this in the world where they were raised. To be who they are, they had to leave. There is no other way to access this internal space.

Those of you who are afraid to escape your glass castle prison are programmed. You know to be in fear of the repercussions if you defect. You must be what somebody needs you to be. The part that boggles my brain is that you are okay with this.

Those of us who were poor scrappy kids who had to find our way through the woods, we got there. It was easy to find out who we were because it was right before us all the time. What you came here to be is right there waiting for you to say "yes" to it. You already know what it is. You know you could easily step into that role as it is what you are made to be or do. But you can't because you will be judged. When we see your perfection moving by, we do not look at you thinking we would want to be you. We see someone so trapped in a reality that we can't imagine how you can find your way out. It would take strength you know you cannot muster.

Could you imagine how pleasant and happy the world would be if everyone in the glass castles came down to the park and took their shoes off? Rather than look at us from your high rise and all you see is our feet getting dirty. Come down and try it. See what it feels like to leave something so high and only man-made, and to touch something made by God.

Feel the planet. When you do, be silent and see what it is saying to you. You don't have to share it with anyone. Just see what it feels like. How does it feel to imagine yourself doing that thing you knew you would do as a child? The course you were set to take until you saw the syllabus of your life. There was no space in between the planning set in place for your life for you to even imagine yourself _____. It would never be accepted in this reality anyway. Why dream?

But you can't stop thinking about it.

To get to it, you'd have to climb through layers of expectations, ingrained training, and the ultimate sacrifice of leaving everyone behind. Why is it hard to leave them? You do know you were brought here as a utility. You are here to serve the needs of the family or ____ where you serve.

I know it's virtually impossible for you to walk away from what you have. But don't you imagine what you would have if you didn't have all of these layers that did not belong to you? You are wearing somebody else's story. How can that feel? There's got to be an inkling of happiness within you.

What makes you happy? I mean to the core where you are bleeding with excitement, happy? The happy that makes you buzz because it feels like your chakras are all lined up and firing all at once. You are spinning at a magnificent energy because everything is in perfect ways. This is what my kind of happy feels like. And it is my way of life. Not a moment passes by when I am not here.

What makes you truly happy? Is it what they told you happiness means to your family?

This is your chance to find out who you are.

When you hear of the ascension, it is about attempting to reach those who have been trained that they are significant. They believe they are more important or "better" than others. They have it engrained in their psyche that they are better and they must be worshipped. It is this self-image that has been created, we are so lost. You have been taught that we have classes and division, and you believe you are at the top of the castle. In your eyes, we are separated by _____. You created this. You were taught, or choose to believe that the one with the most power and money is the one to fear and strive to be like.

To wake up a homeless person who is not strung out is easy. They have nowhere to go but to who they are. You, on the other hand, are more than a challenge. To get you back to your stripped-down version of your original installed software, you have to walk out of a life that does not belong to you. You need to trust and believe that you are enough. You must trust and believe that you did not come here to serve another man. You came here to find your path and to follow it.

By following that which drives your internal freight train heading down a hill, you become what you came here to be. There is no searching for it. It has always been who you are. You just haven't allowed yourself to step into it because you believed others held the key to your life. Now you know better.

By stepping out of the story – no matter what story it is – you are saying "yes" to you. At that moment, you (your higher self) will take over. The work is already done. You already created all of it. All you have to do is like on the Wizard of Oz. Trust in you. Have faith that you did not set yourself up for a lifetime of misery. You had a plan in place that once you find your first breadcrumb, you will begin to feel the power of the tug. You will want to get there because you love how it feels to follow a path created by you.

No one else on this planet could have a clue what your role was to be. We planned it before we were born and everyone had a hand in the planning. But once we become that baby who can't speak, we lose it all. We leave it behind so we can start this journey with a clean slate. At that moment we are a blank canvas. You have the power all lifelong to paint anything you want on your canvas. Or, are you letting someone or something else design your life for you?

In my last book but worthy of repeating. Your mother carried you for nine months (+/-) or you were raised in a tube. No matter how you entered this planet, you came here with programming in place for your desired lessons and destiny. It has to get all muddled because you can't remember.

If you pay attention to nothing but your silent self, the path is presented for you. If you let others tell you what you are to be, you cannot hear it. You are so busy moving into what they want from you, that you can't hear what you are screaming at yourself to hear. The deeper the costume, the harder it is to get out.

Although everyone on the planet has an idea about what you should do, who you should date, where you need to live, and what "job" you should find, they are wrong. Even the person who carried you for nine months, your birth mother, cannot have the slightest clue about what you came here to be. We need to leave each other alone. We each have a plan. No one is special.

There is no judgment at this level. Only at the level of class competition that you have all said it's okay to create.

What you should be scared of, I mean shaking in your boots scared. The more you say "yes" to feeding the power and money in this world, the faster you will see smoke and ash as your future. How did we get to a place where we see those who own everything as the answer? They are gathering up "stuff" because that is all that matters to them. It is the one with the most wins. And you are saying it is okay. Now they own you. You are part of their collection.

You watch the shows about rich people and how horrible they are allowed to be, but you keep watching. The advertisers love you. You wear the clothes they wear. You buy their makeup. The stuff you see the "influencers" of today wearing is all you want. You will sell your child for the right thing. Holy cow the stuff you do to pose for a great selfie with the decorated kids in tow.

How did that get to be significant?

We need to dumb this planet way down and get back to the basics. Level the towers and spread out on the land. Let's share our crops and help each other to find our way back to reality again.

What do we do with the rich and powerful whose children have left them, and they have no one who loves them? They, too are on a journey. It is when we hit our rock bottom that we learn how to bounce. We all have our lows. Once we hit it, there is only one way to go.

You have a journey just as I do. You have something you saw yourself doing as a child. Lean in toward this feeling. See what it was all about. Where will it take you?

When you #STFU and stop trying to be everything for everyone, you can finally introduce yourself to the only one who has ever known what you came here to do. Look in the mirror and say, "Hi _____... today is the first day of the rest of my life. From this moment on, I only listen to me."

THE END

www.ingramcontent.com/pod-product-compliance
Lightning Source LLC
Chambersburg PA
CBHW042028050526
44107CB00103B/732